D1218823

J'AIME LONDON

—

CO-AUTHOR

ROSIE BIRKETT

PHOTOGRAPHY

PIERRE MONETTA

ART DIRECTOR

PIERRE TACHON

—

hardie grant books

MELBOURNE • LONDON

58594
round
the
first time

To Gwénaëlle, who shares my love for London,
and to our children Arzhel and Daé

OFM
BREAKFAST + BURGERS
"the BEST festival food"
→ MIKE SKINNER
@OFMLondon
/OFMLondon
www.originalfryupmaterial.co.uk
Say hi on insta/twit/fb

J'aime London — it's a city that never ceases to amaze me: cosmopolitan, eclectic, vibrant... all at the same time. This culinary guide is my way of offering you a sample of the diverse range of gourmet establishments that have made London's gastronomy scene one of the finest in the world. The last ten years have been revolutionary for this city and have seen the emergence of a harmonious blend of cultures. It has become an incredibly inspirational melting pot for gourmets.

London welcomed me in 2007 for the opening of Alain Ducasse at The Dorchester. It is now my turn to pay tribute to the restaurateurs, producers, and other participants in this world of indulgence, and the culinary artists who do such excellent work there, providing us with a unique experience that is found nowhere else. They know how to showcase their assets: decor, atmosphere, local produce such as game, beef, and seafood from just off the Scottish coast. This, combined with the freedom of spirit that is typical of Londoners, can only add up to remarkable creativity. You will discover all kinds of food, in all kinds of settings: from traditional pub grub to Peruvian restaurants with their delicate ceviches, or a simple sandwich made with Vietnamese bánh mì. I have fond memories of tasting perfectly cooked fish and chips with crisp golden batter, accompanied by minted mushy peas that only the British know how to make; country-style Italian antipasti shared on a restaurant counter, and even a clay-baked beetroot, simply cooked over a wood fire.

All of those moments spent in London bring back a wealth of different emotions that I would like to share with you, by serving London to you on a platter, my way. But this is a mere glimpse into a city that is constantly evolving and changing. And that's why I keep coming back.

ALAIN DUCASSE

CLEANING THE RIVER TOGETHER

As a child growing up in London in the 60s, I remember it being grey, grim and dull and not just on the culinary front. Granted there were a few exclusive eateries, and I was fortunate enough to frequent some as a child, but also part of the joy of being brought up in a French family in London was receiving regular food parcels from relatives such as saucisson a l'ail and perfectly ripe and runny camembert – that was a real treat. Quality produce was hard to come by, and what is now considered common, (and dare I say staples) such as olive oil, farmhouse cheese and artisan bread, was a luxury. As for fruit and vegetables the choice was very basic and quality was more often judged by size rather than taste or gustative value.

Before the reform of the licensing laws, it was at times difficult to get an alcoholic drink, even with a meal. I certainly remember, with some fondness, an Italian restaurant in the Kings Road, pouring from a teapot into a chipped mug, some of the harshest of red wines to accompany my veal Milanese.

How my city has changed. London is now vying with other world capitals to be a gastronomic destination. Tourist used to flock to London to see a show, visit a museum, or watch the ever majestic changing of the guards at Buckingham Palace. But now, as well as that (and more) you can eat well, and food has taken pride of place. London has become a city that is full of brio with taste sensations on every street corner. Michelin-starred chefs rubbing shoulders with the very best of street food, and local eateries opening with gusto. Farmers markets proudly selling beautiful produce and artisan cheese, to go with freshly baked sourdough bread. The melting pot of spices and eclectic cuisines is London's signature dish – so wherever you are at whatever time of day or night, enjoy the delights of London.

I first met Alain Ducasse as a very young commis working for the great chef Alain Chapel in Mionnay. This is where both of us learnt about the respect for ingredients, our love and understanding of true gastronomy. Alain Ducasse has spread his wings and the gospel of taste all over the world including here in London – his eponymous restaurant at the Dorchester is sheer heaven.

MICHEL ROUX

Chef du restaurant Le Gavroche

CON TE NTS

TELEPHONE
TAXI

INSTITUTION
13

INSTITUTION 15

ALAIN DUCASSE AT THE DORCHESTER

53 PARK LANE

MAYFAIR – LONDON, W1K 1QA

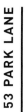

ALAIN DUCASSE AT THE DORCHESTER

53 PARK LANE

MAYFAIR – LONDON, W1K 1QA

ALAIN DUCASSE AT THE DORCHESTER

'Exceptional products, precision and skill. Jocelyn Herland interprets my cuisine for Londoners in a modern and refined style. From melt-in-your-mouth cheese puffs to sauté gourmand of lobster, truffled chicken quenelles and homemade pasta, as well as the Cookpot of seasonal vegetables, Jocelyn cooks every dish to perfection, treating each ingredient with the utmost respect. And my head sommelier Vincent Pastorello's clear advice will help you find the perfect wine to accompany each of the dishes. I wanted this taste experience to take place in a unique setting that made the best use of natural materials. The Table Lumière, the showpiece of the restaurant, treats our guests to an extraordinarily sensory experience, masterfully arranged by my restaurant director Nicolas Defrémont.'

Alain Ducasse

ALAIN DUCASSE AT THE DORCHESTER

53 PARK LANE

MAYFAIR – LONDON, W1K 1QA

BERRY BROS. & RUDD LTD
WINE
BERRY BROS. & RUDD LTD
Wine Merchants
STEWART TURNER
Head Chef
BERRY

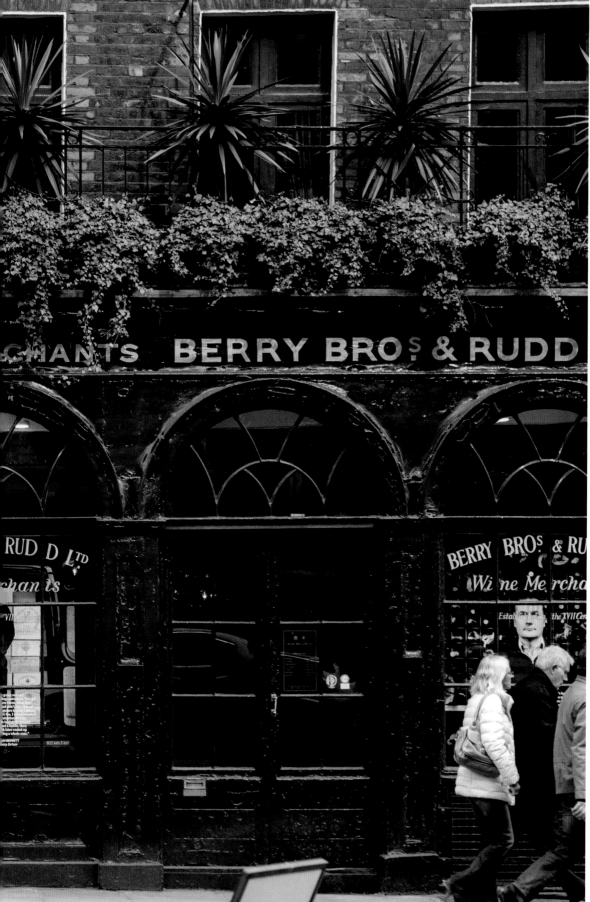

3 ST. JAMES'S STREET

WHITEHALL – LONDON, SW1A 1EG

BERRY BROS & RUDD

THE COFFEE MILL

1935
BRETZENHEIMER
AUF DES HOLLE,
NAHE

BERRY BROS & RUDD

The dark painted exterior of Britain's most historic wine merchant belies the two acres of labyrinthine cellars that sprawl beneath. Inside the rickety, wood-panelled Mayfair premises, from which the company has traded since the 17th century, you can explore not just the world of fine wine, but Britain's history. Relics on display include: a letter from the Titanic (the merchant lost six cases when it sank); the original scales used to weigh its customers for 150 years; and a miniature wine collection that was created for Queen Mary's doll's house. The family company has held a royal warrant since the reign of King George III, but it's anything but archaic – having been the first wine merchant to open an online shop in 1994. Nothing beats an actual visit to the original townhouse, where the knowledgeable staff will find whatever wine you're after – be it a £13 Picpoul or a £13,000 Romanée Conti.

Breakfast
Club
hoxton
ORIGINAL
HP
SAUCE

2-4 RUFUS STREET

HOXTON – LONDON, N1 6PE

BREAKFAST CLUB (THE)

PINGOUIN

24 HR
CARGO
Corona
Extra

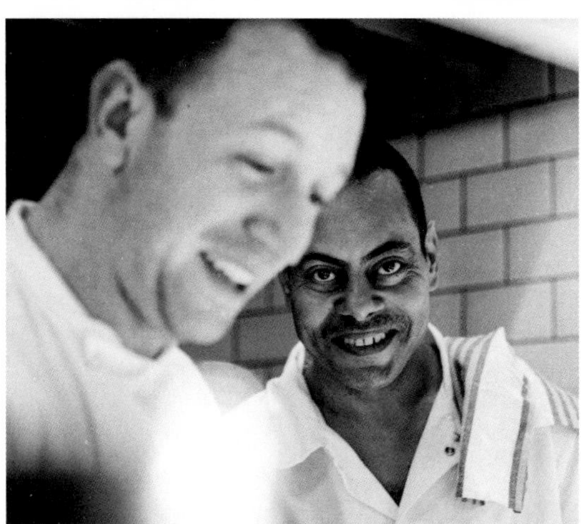

MET A STRANGE LADY

AT
MAJOR
ROAD
AHEAD
BOYS &
Girls
LOUIS SEYFRIED
LYONS

THE BREAKFAST CLUB

Children of the 1980s, and anyone else with a marked appreciation of 'the shoulder pad years', find a happy haven in this Hoxton outpost of the American-diner-meets-British-greasy-spoon cafe. Having started in Soho and expanded all over London, the people behind this quirky mini-group have stayed true to what originally made them such a hit – big, bolstering breakfasts and lunches eaten inside a fun, kinetic cocoon of kitsch memorabilia. This East End site is bigger than the others, but is still packed with 1980s treasures that woo retro junkies, like a Mickey Mouse statuette and an archaic TV. That woo retro-junkies. Living up to its name, breakfast is still the main draw; try the wicked breakfast burrito of chorizo, scrambled egg, guacamole, Cheddar and spicy pepper sauce.

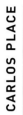

CONNAUGHT (THE)

CARLOS PLACE

MAYFAIR – LONDON, W1K 2AL

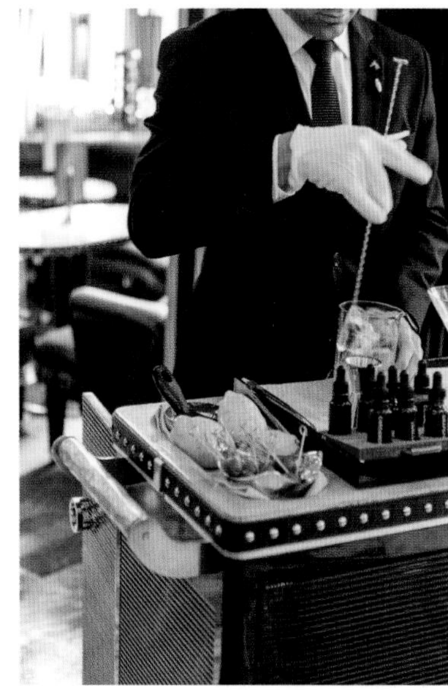

THE CONNAUGHT

Amidst all its elegance and refinement, a brilliantly bacchanalian spirit pervades this iconic Mayfair hotel, thanks to its distinguished food and drink offerings. Its two bars, The Connaught and The Coburg, are deluxe drinking dens with impressive selections of vintages, limited-edition champagnes and world-famous cocktails served in smart, elegant surroundings. French two-star Michelin chef Hélène Darroze has a gastronomic restaurant in the hotel, and is also responsible for the breakfast, lunch and tapas menu at The Coburg. At The Connaught, the martini, made with crispy Gancia Dry vermouth from Italy, is so famous it warrants its own trolley: complete with glass phials of different extracts like cardamom, ginger and grapefruit to make your cocktail even more memorable.

RTNUM & MASON PLC

181 PICCADILLY

PICCADILLY – LONDON, W1A 1ER

FORTNUM & MASON

FORTNUM & MASON

Strong links to the East India Company when it was just a grocer in the 1700s ensured this quintessentially British department store's trailblazing access to rare, quality teas and spices. To this day, the Piccadilly stalwart is the go-to place for everything from artisan British produce, like Herefordshire Ragstone goat's cheese and hand-raised pork pies made with outdoor-bred Lincolnshire pork, to its weird and wonderful preserves, like unripe hedgerow blackberries in cider vinegar or 'fig cheese', and its homemade biscuits, chocolates, macarons and sumptuous hampers. The Diamond Jubilee Tea Salon – which was opened with a visit from the Queen in 2012 – is one of the best places in the capital to take afternoon tea, with its extensive list that includes premium-grade orange pekoe and first flush leaf teas.

FORTNUM & MASON

181 PICCADILLY

PICCADILLY – LONDON, W1A 1ER

WINDOWS

26 SOUTH AUDLEY STREET

MAYFAIR – LONDON W1K 2PD

HARRY'S BAR

26 SOUTH AUDLEY STREET
MAYFAIR – LONDON W1K 2PD

HARRY'S BAR

Members or guests at this Mayfair institution get a secret glimpse into London's glamorous past every time they ring the doorbell. This place has been going since 1979, and still attracts the old-school crowd, but to call it a 'bar' is a bit misleading. While you can enjoy crumbling chunks of 24-month-aged Parmigiana Reggiano, Sicilian bread and Bellinis at the shiny marble bar, this place is as much about the dining room, which hangs with glittering chandeliers and the works of Peter Arno and other *New Yorker* artists. Impeccable, authentic northern Italian food is the offering here, and the Piedmont beef carpaccio with garden pea sauce is a favourite.

La Petite Maison
tous célèbres ici
La Petite Maison

LA PETITE MAISON

53-54 BROOK'S MEWS

MAYFAIR – LONDON, W1K 4EG

FANTASTIQUE
fantastic place
Best wishes
Amazing Service
WILL BE BACK!
good luck
Fantastic Carike!

LA PETITE MAISON

‘When I went to the restaurant in Nice, the dish which won me over was the warm prawns in olive oil. It’s so simple – just prawns, olive oil, lemon juice and basil – but it’s awesome, and I knew I could build a menu around that,’ says chef patron Raphael Duntoye, who brought the light, olive oil-bathed cuisine of Côte d’Azur to Mayfair when he opened the London cousin of the legendary Nice restaurant in 2007. Previously head chef at Zuma and alumni of Pierre Koffmann, Duntoye has crafted a restaurant that rings with Riviera bonhomie in the midst of Mayfair – its tables laid with lemons, ripe tomatoes and bottles of olive oil. Finely sliced octopus, set with its own gelatine, is drizzled with garlicky lemon oil, and melts on the tongue; slivers of marinated scallop are studded with jewels of cranberry and given crunchy depth by toasted flaked almonds. ‘I want you to have the first bite and not be able to wait to have the second bite, and to share various plates. This is how food should be. It should be fun. It should be like a journey.’

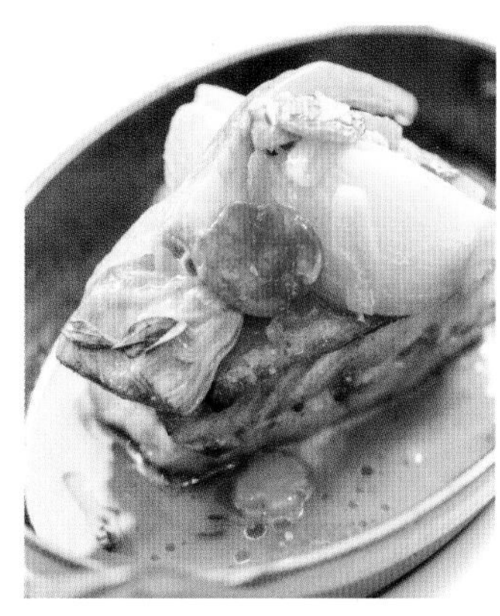

EBURY STREET SW1
CITY OF WESTMINSTER
LA PO LE AU POT

INSTITUTION 49

LA POULE AU POT

231 EBURY STREET

BELGRAVIA – LONDON, SW1W 8UT

INSTITUTION 51

231 EBURY STREET
BELGRAVIA – LONDON, SW1W 8UT

LA POULE AU POT

Unashamedly eccentric, with its stage-set interior of plastic grapes, wicker baskets and candelabras, this Belgravia bistro is a rare time warp on a restaurant landscape defined by reinvention. Having remained almost unchanged since it opened in the 1960s, it's the kind of place you'll find couples who first came here 40 years ago reliving the romance alongside French expats looking for a taste of home. And, boy, do they find it in the proudly French-only written menus, the buttery, garlic-laden escargots and heady, fish-stock-rich soupe de poisson. The three-course table d'hôte lunch menu is incredible value; though choosing between the Toulouse sausage and steak frites is not an easy decision for any Francophile to make.

LEDBURY (THE)

127 LEDBURY ROAD

NOTTING HILL – LONDON, W11 2AQ

INSTITUTION 53

THE LEDBURY

Far from the madding-central-London-chef-crowd, on a serene street in leafiest Notting Hill, Australian-born chef Brett Graham has been quietly turning out some of London's most exceptional and exciting fine dining fare since 2005. Having previously worked under one of the capital's most cherished and respected chefs — Philip Howard at The Square — Graham's gone on to achieve the elusive accolade also held by his former mentor in the form of two glittering Michelin stars. He has a way with British ingredients that delights visually, intellectually and culinarily; while rooted in the classics, his food harnesses a refreshing lightness and modernity. Inside The Ledbury's simple, sophisticated dining room it's the food, not the 'concept' or decor, that does the talking — along with the amenable and knowledgeable staff. A dish of deeply savoury grilled onion broth with subtle buffalo milk curds and Saint-Nectaire and truffle toast is sublime, balanced and somehow nostalgic — French onion soup and cheese on toast lurking on the peripheries of its conception. Berkshire muntjac deer comes moist, rare and tender on a bed of ruby-red beetroot, endive, radicchio and cherry blossoms, with two pearls of buttery bone marrow on top.

127 LEDBURY ROAD

NOTTING HILL – LONDON, W11 2AQ

LEDBURY (THE)

INSTITUTION 57

LE GAVROCHE

43 UPPER BROOK STREET

MAYFAIR – LONDON W1K 7QR

LE GAVROCHE

43 UPPER BROOK STREET
MAYFAIR – LONDON W1K 7QR

Heston Blumenthal has compared the impact of the Roux brothers on British gastronomy to that of The Beatles on pop music, and the epoch-defining influence the French brothers would have on UK dining all started with the launch of Le Gavroche in 1967. Fast-forward almost half a century, and the Mayfair restaurant is still a beacon of fine dining in the capital, with Michel Roux Jr having taken over the restaurant from his father Albert in 1991. This is a place for special-occasion meals, and attention to gastronomic detail is everywhere – from the toque-hatted chef cutlery, to the perfect intricate canapés, exceptionally crafted dishes and beautiful petits fours. The restaurant's signature cheese soufflé – a mixture of Gruyère and Cheddar, swimming in a rich bath of cream – sums this place up: generous, delicious and exquisitely indulgent.

PROMENADE AT THE DORCHESTER (THE)

53 PARK LANE

MAYFAIR – LONDON, W1K 1QA

STEINWAY &

THE PROMENADE AT THE DORCHESTER

53 PARK LANE
MAYFAIR – LONDON, W1K 1QA

At the Dorchester, afternoon tea is still what this most elegant of English rituals should be: an unapologetically lavish, deliciously tradition-steeped three-course affair. Fine china and white linen are a given. Champagne is optional – though bubbles suit the mood of such a grand setting, amidst soaring marble pillars and towering palms in 'The Promenade' lobby of this legendary Mayfair hotel. Settle into the sumptuous, pristinely upholstered furniture and prepare to be beguiled by this gracious service, which begins with carefully filled crustless sandwiches, accompanied by your tea of choice – be it smokey Lapsang Souchon or fragrant Earl Grey. Warm scones made to a recipe unchanged for over half a century follow. Slather on the strawberry jam and Devonshire clotted cream, but save room for the pièce de resistance – the pastry platter: an immaculately crafted parade of delightful treats including white chocolate and praline pyramids, mini raspberry macaroons, perfect pineapple financiers and a creamy apple and macadamia delice.

QUO VADIS
RESTAUR

QUO VADIS

26-29 DEAN STREET

SOHO – LONDON, W1D 3LL

QV
BAR
BIRRA
BAR
QV

26-29 DEAN STREET

SOHO – LONDON, W1D 3LL

QUO VADIS

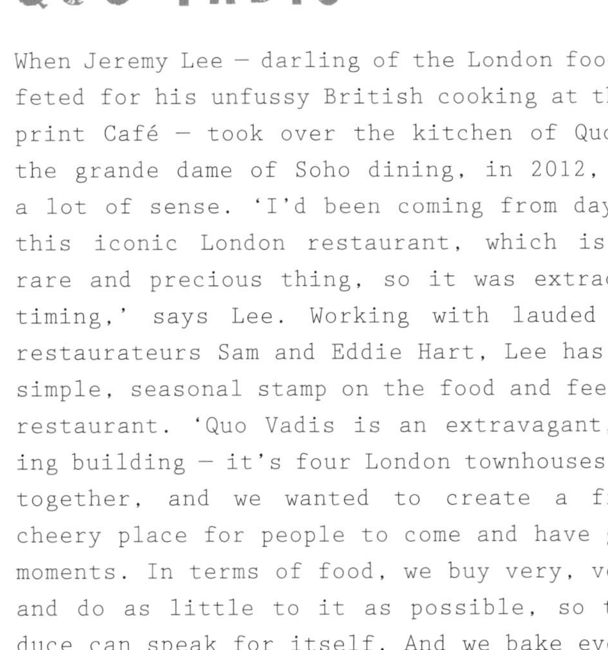

When Jeremy Lee – darling of the London food scene, feted for his unfussy British cooking at the Blueprint Café – took over the kitchen of Quo Vadis, the grande dame of Soho dining, in 2012, it made a lot of sense. 'I'd been coming from day one to this iconic London restaurant, which is a very rare and precious thing, so it was extraordinary timing,' says Lee. Working with lauded brother restaurateurs Sam and Eddie Hart, Lee has put his simple, seasonal stamp on the food and feel of the restaurant. 'Quo Vadis is an extravagant, imposing building – it's four London townhouses knocked together, and we wanted to create a friendly, cheery place for people to come and have gorgeous moments. In terms of food, we buy very, very well and do as little to it as possible, so the produce can speak for itself. And we bake everything ourselves in the bakery downstairs. Our mantra is: "if we can't make it, we don't sell it".'

RIVER CAFE (THE)

THAMES WHARF, RAINVILLE ROAD

HAMMERSMITH – LONDON, W6 9HA

INSTITUTION 69

THE RIVER CAFE

Down by the river, inside a long, light room, well-heeled Londoners come together to eat Italian food that's been setting standards for its quality and unapologetic simplicity for over 25 years. A few perch at the bar with a spritz and a plate of the signature chargrilled squid with chilli and rocket, but most settle in at one of the tables and feast for hours on sublime plates of artichoke with explosively creamy burrata, glossy spaghetti vongole and wood-oven roasted Dover sole that is soft, sweet and sharpened with capers, lemon and parsley. During service the room fills with the sound only the best restaurants make — that buzz of laughter, cutlery, plates, glasses and chat. It's the hum of happiness: something the late Rose Gray and Ruth Rogers, who still works the pass, brought to London in spades in 1987, when they set up their kitchen that would go on to train the likes of Jamie Oliver, Theo Randall, April Bloomfield and Hugh Fearnley Whittingstall.

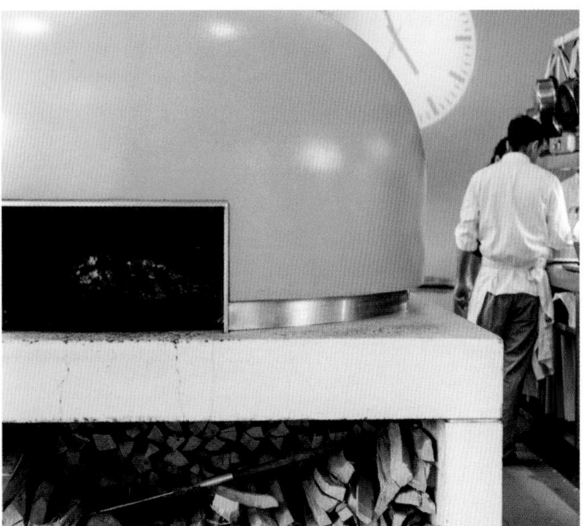

RIVER CAFE (THE)

THAMES WHARF, RAINVILLE ROAD

HAMMERSMITH – LONDON, W6 9HA

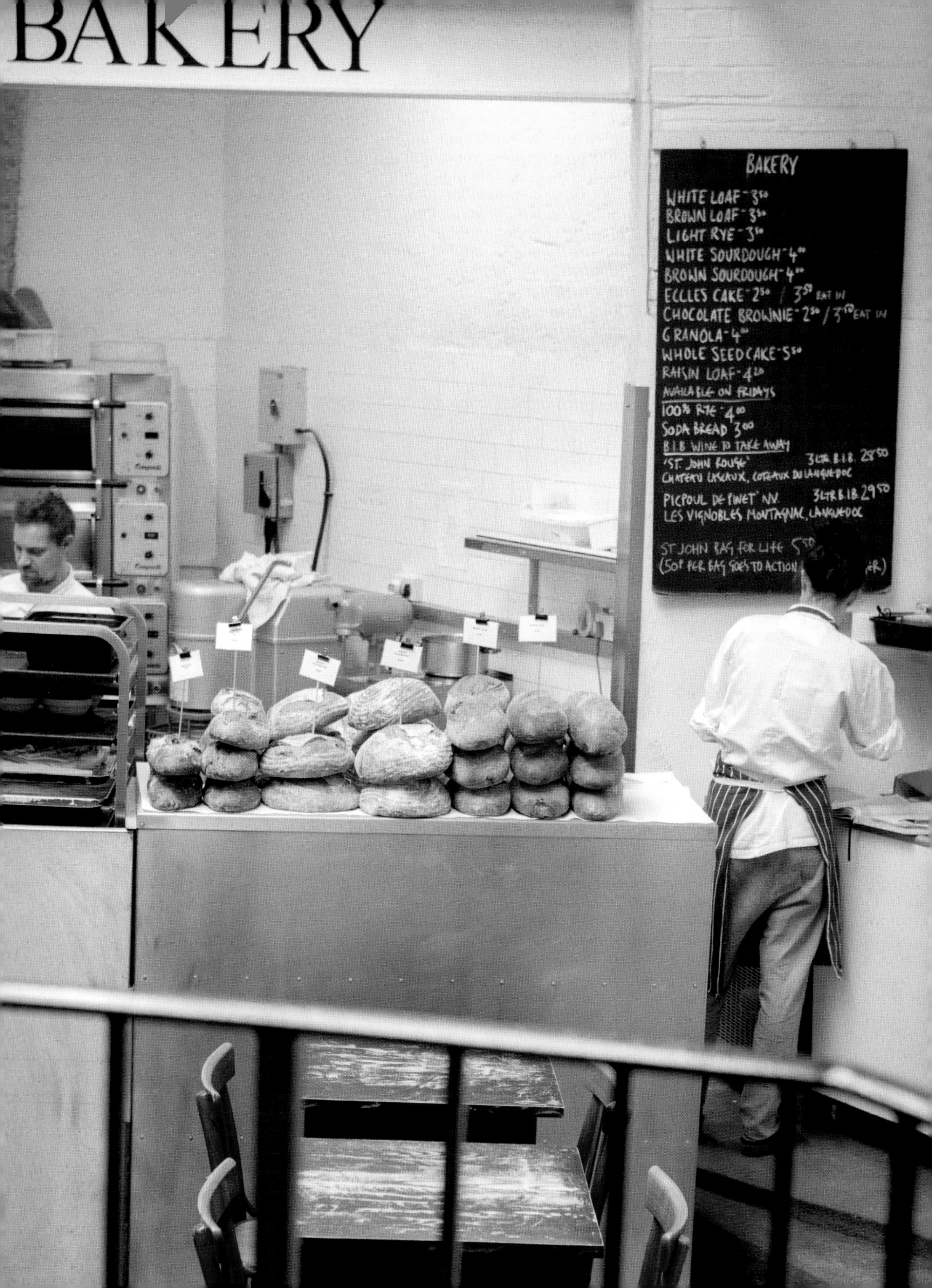
BAKERY
BAKERY
WHITE LOAF - 3^{50}
BROWN LOAF - 3^{50}
LIGHT RYE - 3^{50}
WHITE SOURDOUGH - 4^{00}
BROWN SOURDOUGH - 4^{00}
ECCLES CAKE - 2^{50} / 3^{50} EAT IN
CHOCOLATE BROWNIE - 2^{50} / 3^{50} EAT IN
GRANOLA - 4^{00}
WHOLE SEED CAKE - 5^{50}
RAISIN LOAF - 4^{20}
AVAILABLE ON FRIDAYS
100% RYE - 4^{00}
SODA BREAD 3^{00}
B.I.B WINE TO TAKE AWAY
'ST. JOHN ROUGE' 3LTR. B.I.B. 28^{50}
CHATEAU LASCAUX, COTEAUX DU LANGUEDOC
PICPOUL DE PINET NV. 3LTR B.I.B. 29^{50}
LES VIGNOBLES MONTAGNAC, LANGUEDOC
ST JOHN BAG FOR LIFE 5^{50}
(50P PER BAG GOES TO ACTION

ST. JOHN

26 ST. JOHN STREET

CLERKENWELL – LONDON, EC1M 4AY

St. JOHN
BREAD and WINE
TAURANT • BAKERY • WINE SHOP

26 ST. JOHN STREET

CLERKENWELL – LONDON, EC1M 4AY

ST. JOHN

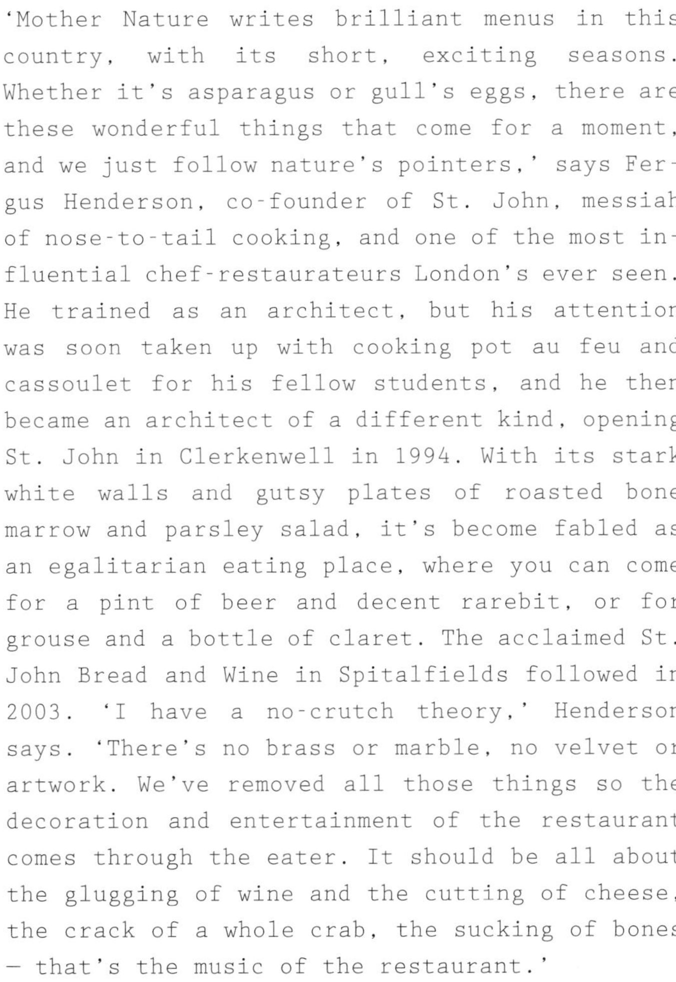

'Mother Nature writes brilliant menus in this country, with its short, exciting seasons. Whether it's asparagus or gull's eggs, there are these wonderful things that come for a moment, and we just follow nature's pointers,' says Fergus Henderson, co-founder of St. John, messiah of nose-to-tail cooking, and one of the most influential chef-restaurateurs London's ever seen. He trained as an architect, but his attention was soon taken up with cooking pot au feu and cassoulet for his fellow students, and he then became an architect of a different kind, opening St. John in Clerkenwell in 1994. With its stark white walls and gutsy plates of roasted bone marrow and parsley salad, it's become fabled as an egalitarian eating place, where you can come for a pint of beer and decent rarebit, or for grouse and a bottle of claret. The acclaimed St. John Bread and Wine in Spitalfields followed in 2003. 'I have a no-crutch theory,' Henderson says. 'There's no brass or marble, no velvet or artwork. We've removed all those things so the decoration and entertainment of the restaurant comes through the eater. It should be all about the glugging of wine and the cutting of cheese, the crack of a whole crab, the sucking of bones – that's the music of the restaurant.'

INSTITUTION

77

160 PICCADILLY

PICCADILLY – LONDON, W1J 9EB

WOLSELEY (THE)

囍
福
福
囍

160 PICCADILLY

PICCADILLY – LONDON, W1J 9EB

THE WOLSELEY

Breakfasting at Chris Corbin and Jeremy King's grand European 'Cafe' in Mayfair has become a legendary dining ritual that counts celebrities, influencers and culinary movers and shakers among its denizens. There's just something about the soaring vaulted ceilings, black and white marble floor and tables of fresh pastries that sets this former automotive showroom and bank apart. Accessible glamour is the modus operandi, and the surprisingly egalitarian brasserie menu offers everything from a humble but perfectly crispy bacon roll, to the famous omelette Arnold Bennett: an opulent confluence of smoked haddock, cream and hollandaise. It will keep you going until supper, when you might just find yourself back there to get cosy with a very good wiener schnitzel...

ZUMA

5 RAPHAEL STREET

KNIGHTSBRIDGE – LONDON, SW7 IDL

ZUMA

Over a decade since it opened its doors, chef Rainer Becker and businessman Arjun Waney's original restaurant collaboration in Knightsbridge – which has since expanded to as far afield as Miami and Bangkok – is still one of London's hottest culinary tickets. Having spent six years ensconced in the Tokyo food scene, working at the Park Hyatt hotel and acquiring an intimate knowledge of Japanese dining rituals and methods, Becker created something unique when he opened this relaxed, upscale playground for hungry, urbane Londoners. This is where media darlings, business suits, Japanese food junkies and restaurant obsessives looking for a slice of Tokyo pie come to feast; and the food doesn't disappoint, with clean, punchy flavours in stalwarts like the sliced sea bass with yuzu, truffle oil and salmon roe, or the spicy beef tenderloin with sesame, red chilli and sweet soy. Loosely based on izakaya – Japan's more informal dining experience – the restaurant has a cool, relaxed vibe that's enhanced by its sleek, natural design, with earth-tone granite, Japanese rice-paper panels and imported Indonesian wooden tables.

ZUMA

5 RAPHAEL STREET

KNIGHTSBRIDGE – LONDON, SW7 IDL

PLACE TO BE
85

ALBION

2-4 BOUNDARY STREET

SHOREDITCH – LONDON E2 7DD

ALBION

ALBION

Terence Conran and Peter Prescott's stylish, airy cafe-cum-bakery and deli prides itself on the Britishness of its setting, ingredients and recipes. Located in the former Victorian warehouse which also houses their Boundary boutique hotel in Shoreditch, it's a cool, clean, all-day dining space in which to enjoy everything from a sausage sandwich or oysters and Bloody Marys — to hearty heritage dishes like rabbit stew. If you're just passing through the neighbourhood, it's worth popping in to pick up a loaf of sourdough from the award-winning bakery or to try one of the baked products created by the in-house pastry chefs.

ALBION

2-4 BOUNDARY STREET

SHOREDITCH – LONDON E2 7DD

4-6 RUSSELL STREET

COVENT GARDEN – LONDON, WC2B 5HZ

BALTHAZAR

Porridge

4-6 RUSSELL STREET
COVENT GARDEN – LONDON, WC2B 5HZ

BALTHAZAR

Keith McNally has been many things in his life – a scene-defining restaurateur in New York being the most obvious (though he's also acted in, and directed films) – but he was born a Londoner, and in 2013 he returned to bring his Big Apple baby home. Balthazar – his Parisian-style brasserie behemoth – landed spectacularly, and suitably theatrically, in Covent Garden, opening in a grand room with leather banquettes, enormous mirrors and whirring ceiling fans that make it seem as ancient as its antique fixtures suggest. It's every bit as glamorous as its New York cousin, and in the kinetic 170-seat dining room, plates of French brasserie fare with a slight New York accent are devoured by dine-hard devotees. At the 26-foot pewter bar, cocktails are mixed just as you like them and might precede a curly endive salad, dressed lusciously with bacon-shallot vinaigrette and a soft poached egg sprawling its silky yolk over the top. Main courses might mean brasserie stalwarts like lapin à la moutarde with spaetzle, or more modern interpretations like the umami-rich duck shepherd's pie.

BARBECOA

20 NEW CHANGE PASSAGE

ST PAUL'S – LONDON, EC4M 9AG

BARBECOA

London's love affair with barbecue stepped up a notch when golden boy Jamie Oliver opened his firepit fantasy restaurant in 2010. Floor-to-ceiling windows overlooking St Paul's Cathedral add a certain drama to this industrial-chic inferno, where kitchens celebrate the various forms of traditional, fire-based cooking methods: sporting a Texas pit smoker, tandoors, robata grills and wood-fired ovens. Before being expertly flame-licked, the meat here is hand-picked by the restaurant's butchers to ensure quality, while beef is dry-aged in-house for anything up to 70 days to enhance the flavour. While carnivores fawn over plates of pulled pork, baby back ribs and crispy pigs cheeks, Prosecco cocktails like the 'Death in The Afternoon', made with Pernod, absinthe and lemon, ensure it's not a purely butch affair.

20 NEW CHANGE PASSAGE

ST PAUL'S – LONDON, EC4M 9AG

LASSCO

PLACE TO BE 99

BRUNSWICK HOUSE CAFÉ

30 WANDSWORTH ROAD

VAUXHALL – LONDON, SW8 2LG

BRUNSWICK HOUSE CAFÉ

'Brunswick House started as a ten-seat espresso and sandwich bar. Between my brother Frank and I, we had a cool £2000 saved up from tips, with which we leased a coffee machine, bought some mugs, and struck a deal with Lassco, the London architectural salvage institution who had bought and restored this beautiful 18th-century mansion house in Vauxhall. We agreed we'd rent the floor space and they'd keep the walls and ceilings from which to hang antique panelling, chandeliers – all manner of beautiful gear. It was our simple goal to combine focused seasonal cooking with a culture of old-fashioned hospitality and occasion appropriate to such a fabulous setting. The restaurant has slowly expanded over the last three years, and now comfortably seats 80. The fish we're getting from Cornwall at the moment is unparalleled – it really makes one happy to be alive.'

Jackson Boxer

PLACE TO BE
101

BRUNSWICK HOUSE CAFÉ

30 WANDSWORTH ROAD

VAUXHALL – LONDON, SW8 2LG

bubbledogs
70

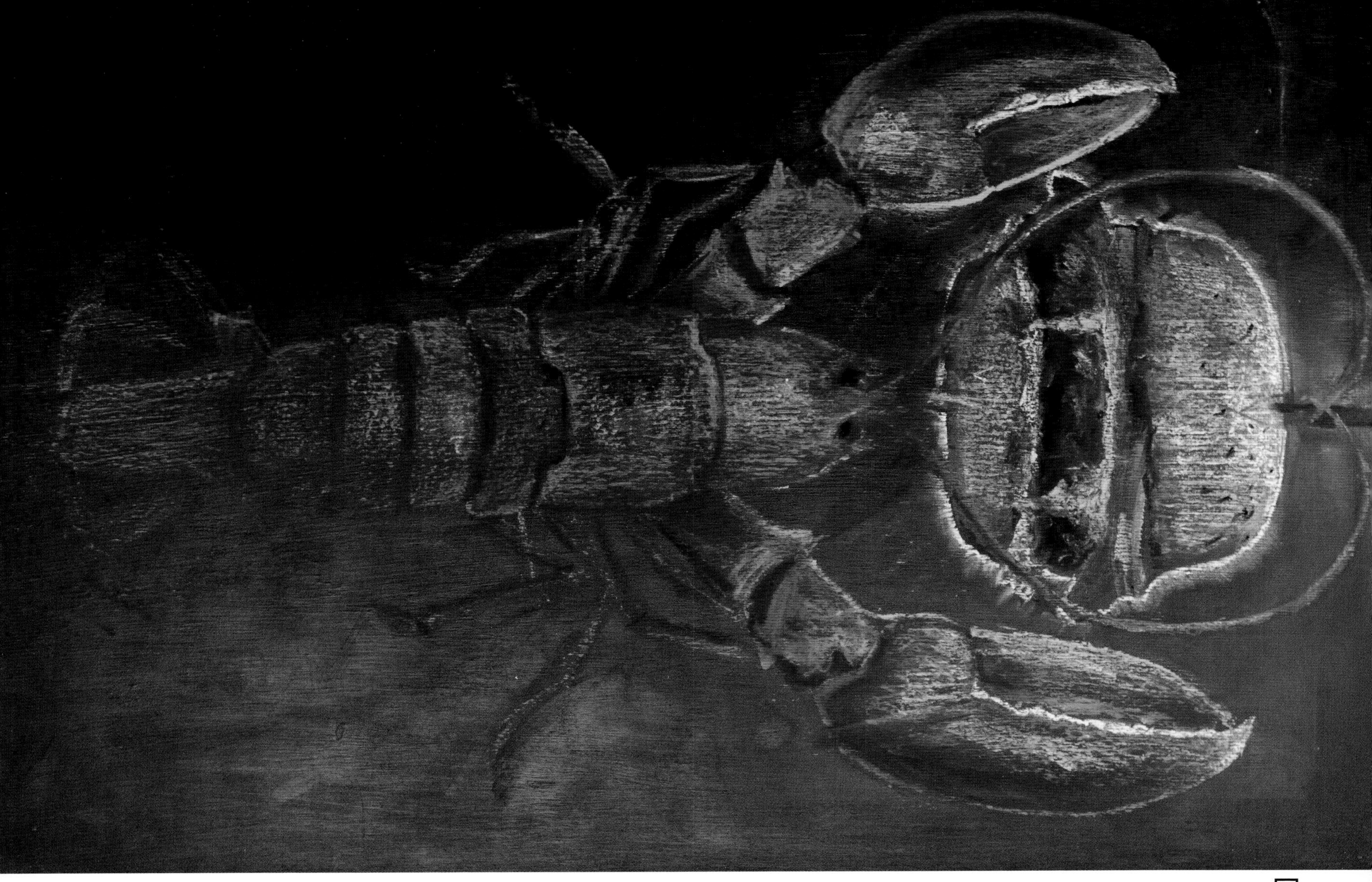

BURGER AND LOBSTER

29 CLARGES STREET
MAYFAIR – LONDON, W1J 7EF

PLACE TO BE
107

BURGER AND LOBSTER

Surf or turf — the choice is yours. Although, there's nothing stopping you from ordering all of the menu items on offer at this vibey, original Mayfair outpost of the Burger and Lobster mini-group. After all, there are only three options, and they each cost just £20. Pick from a juicy, sweet steamed Canadian lobster that has the option to be finished on a charcoal grill with butter sauce; a moist, 10-ounce ground-beef patty sandwiched between a home-made sesame bun; or a soft, sumptuous brioche encasing mayonnaise-swathed lobster meat, topped with a fresh claw. This place has made an art out of simplicity, serving each item with golden, crunchy fries and a salad. Washing it all down with one of the signature Soul Shakers' cocktails is a very good idea. Try the 'Riesling Smash', a heady mix of Riesling, apricots, pink grapefruit and Kammerling's ginseng spirit.

BURGER AND LOBSTER

29 CLARGES STREET

MAYFAIR – LONDON, W1J 7EF

CARAVAN
securifix
ALCOHOL CONTROL ZONE
PLEASE USE THE SIDE ENTRANCE
pashley

CARAVAN

11-13 EXMOUTH MARKET

CAMDEN – LONDON, EC1R 4QD

COFFEE MENU

CARAVA
DRINK MENU

11-13 EXMOUTH MARKET
CAMDEN – LONDON, EC1R 4QD

CARAVAN

There are few things that could kick-start any food-lover's weekend more pleasurably than brunch at this thriving, breezy Antipodean restaurant, bar and coffee roastery in culinarily cool Exmouth Market. Thick slices of grilled coconut bread topped with lemon curd-flavoured cream cheese and – depending on the season – the ripest, sweetest strawberries or rhubarb is one way to soak up the brilliance of this globe-trotting menu. Cornbread French toast with maple syrup, rocket, bacon and avocado is another. Coffee to accompany such delights is roasted downstairs, at the on-site roastery, and is also supplied to restaurants and cafes around London. During the week, attentions turn to the fusion-focused sharing-plates menu, where you might find an expertly seared onglet with miso, green beans and peanut dressing to soak up your martini made with Sipsmith gin, earl grey, lemon and egg white.

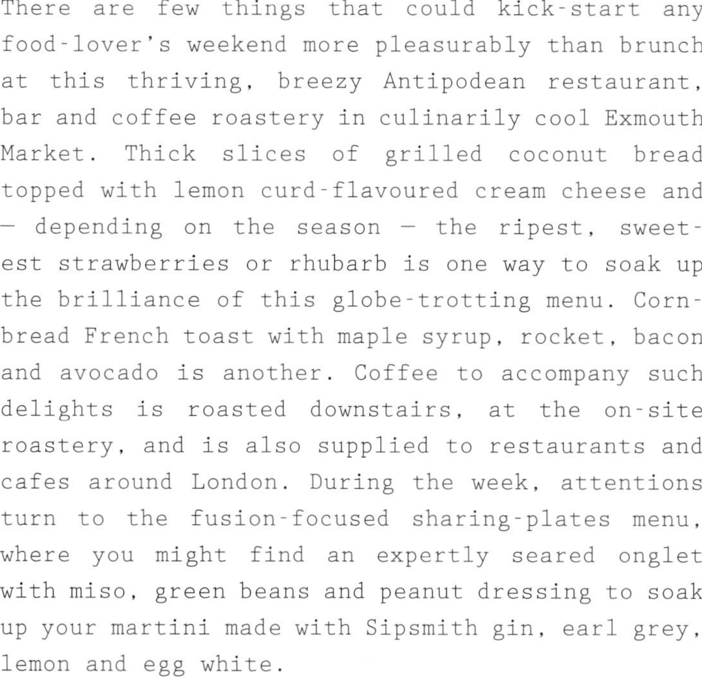

Display ticket
Max stay 4 hours

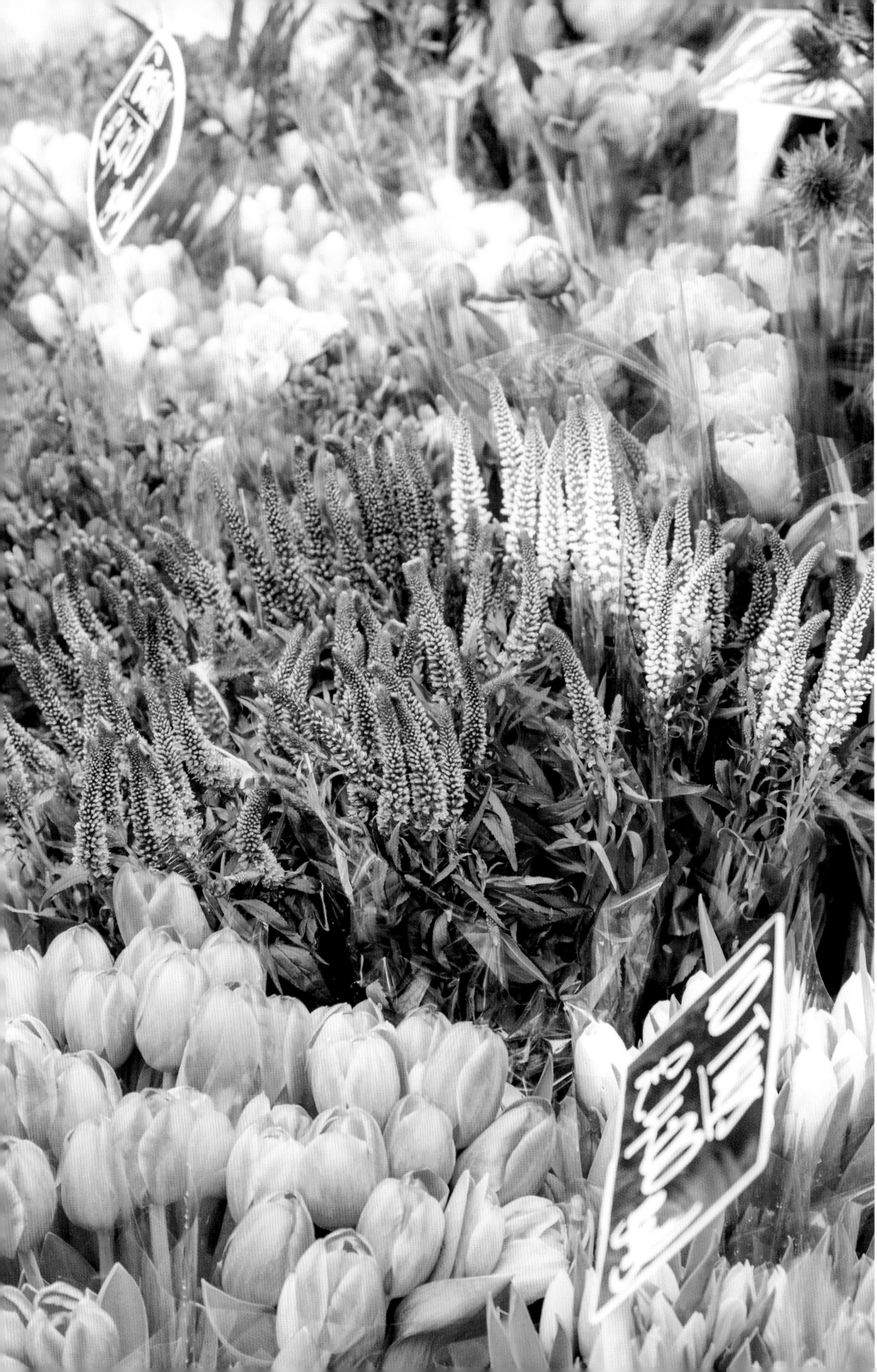

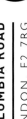

COLUMBIA ROAD FLOWER MARKET

2 FOR
£5.00
£3.00

COLUMBIA ROAD FLOWER MARKET

Hipsters, tourists and locals collide at this East End street market every Sunday between 8am and 3pm, to lose themselves in the jungle of lilies, daffodils, roses, chrysanthemums and other cut flowers and foliage. Originally a Saturday food market set up in 1869, it moved to Sundays to accommodate its Jewish traders, and became a hub for Covent Garden and Spitalfields traders to sell their leftover cut-flower stock. These days the market is surrounded by over 60 independent shops and art galleries, and, in keeping with its Victorian heritage as a food market, it teems with artisan eateries like miniature bakery Lily Vanilli, where you'll find creative, daringly decorated cakes strewn with chocolate shards and edible flowers, and seasonal frangipane tarts.

DABBOUS

39 WHITFIELD STREET

FITZROVIA – LONDON, WIT 2SF

DABBOUS

'The primary objective was to still be open after year one,' says Ollie Dabbous, the young chef behind one of London's most fervently received, scene-shifting restaurants. 'We had no money when we opened, but we always envisaged offering a good night out, as opposed to just dinner. I wanted it to be stripped-back fine dining without the fuss, and to have a sociable bar aligned with the restaurant. We also wanted somewhere devoid of any ceremony or self-importance, where people would feel immediately at ease.' Dabbous' creative, natural cuisine — dishes such as iced sorrel with peas and mint, or mixed alliums in a chilled pine broth — elevates ordinary ingredients into something very special. 'We just try to make the food taste as good as it can, in the most organic way.'

39 WHITFIELD STREET

FITZROVIA – LONDON, WIT 2SF

DABBOUS

PLACE TO BE
123

DEAN STREET TOWNHOUSE

69-71 DEAN STREET

SOHO – LONDON, WID 3SE

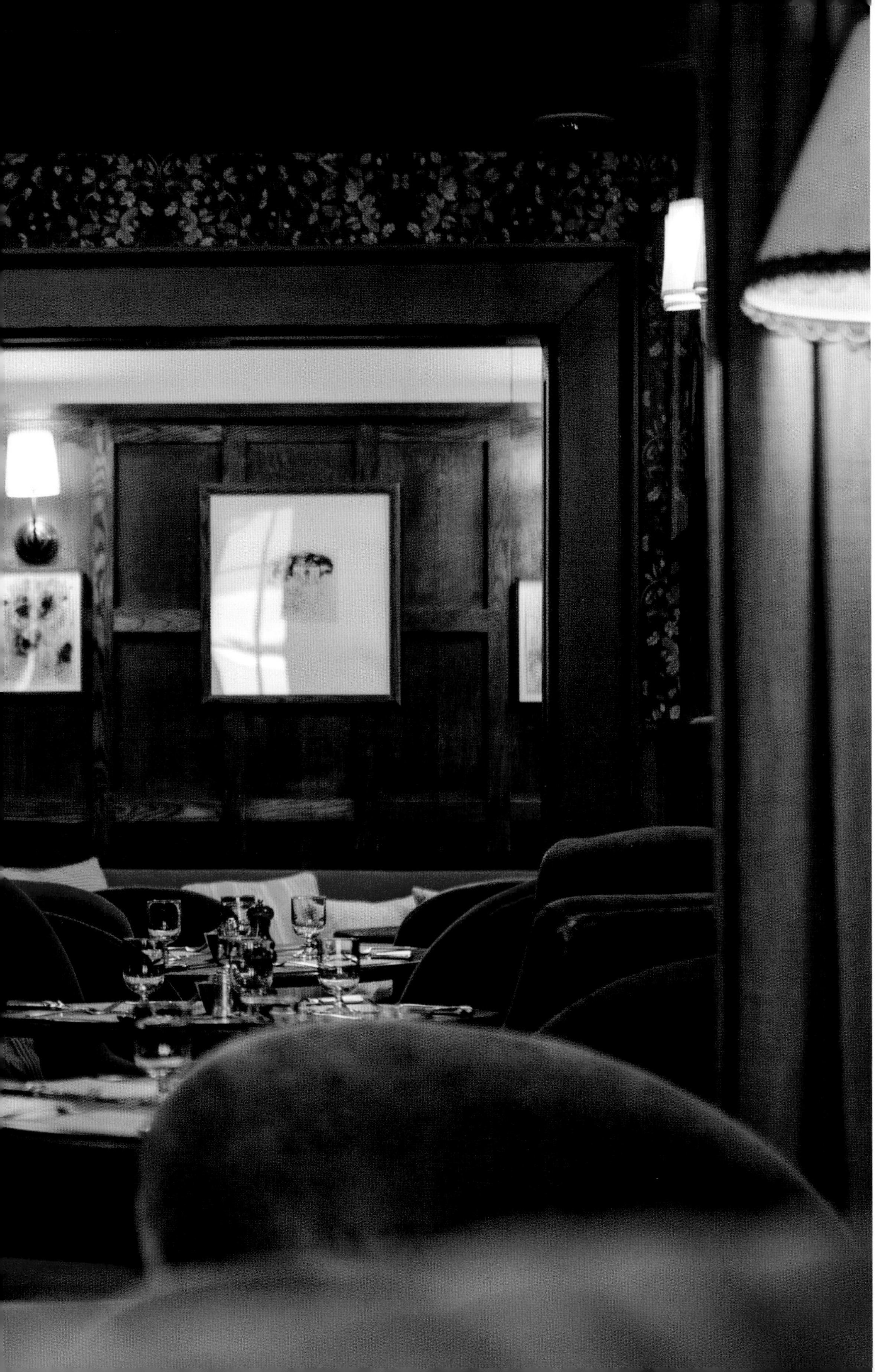

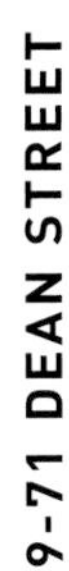

THE ANATOMY OF THE BEAST

PLACE TO BE
125

69-71 DEAN STREET
SOHO – LONDON, W1D 3SE

DEAN STREET TOWNHOUSE

Though a hip all-day hangout and boutique hotel, this place comes alive for breakfast, lunch and dinner, sucking in the workers and characters of Soho with its speakeasy-style cocktails and unfussy British food. As you might expect from the minds behind media-darling member's club Soho House, there's an easy, undulating cool to the place – from the hanging Tracey Emins to the prohibition-styled bar staff, who mix creative, quenching tinctures like celery gimlets from behind their beards. Food celebrates seasonal native produce and British culinary heritage, appealing to both the comfort eater and bon viveur in dishes like the homely mince and buttered potatoes and the sea trout with buttered peas, lettuce and lovage.

PLACE TO BE
127

ELECTRIC DINER

191 PORTOBELLO ROAD
NOTTING HILL – LONDON, W11 2ED

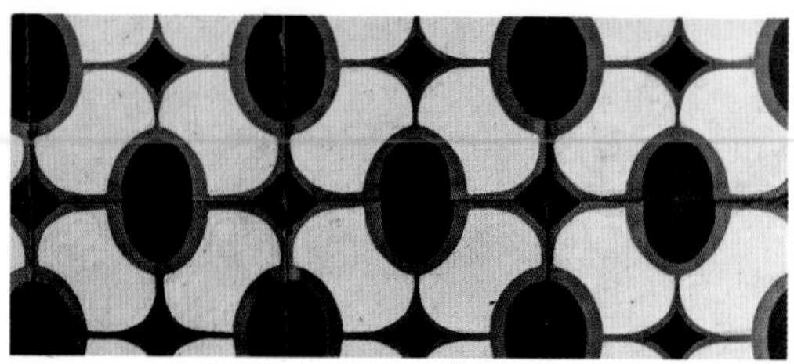

ELECTRIC DINER

Brendan Sodikoff, the chef behind Chicago's feted Au Cheval French-American diner, is one of a clutch of US chefs to cotton on to London's love of his country's pimped-up junk food and bring it over for our enjoyment. Along with the minds behind Soho House, he opened this cool, exposed-brick, red leather banquette-clad all-day hangout in 2013, adjacent to the famous Electric Cinema in deepest Notting Hill. Like Au Cheval, the menu is French-American, featuring creations like his famous bologna sandwich, a concoction of fried bologna piled high upon itself, moist and crispy, sandwiched between buttery brioche with a big, fat pickle. The lush bone marrow with beef-cheek marmalade is also an instant classic, but those looking for something a little more saintly will find solace in cleaner dishes like sea bass with capers and lemon.

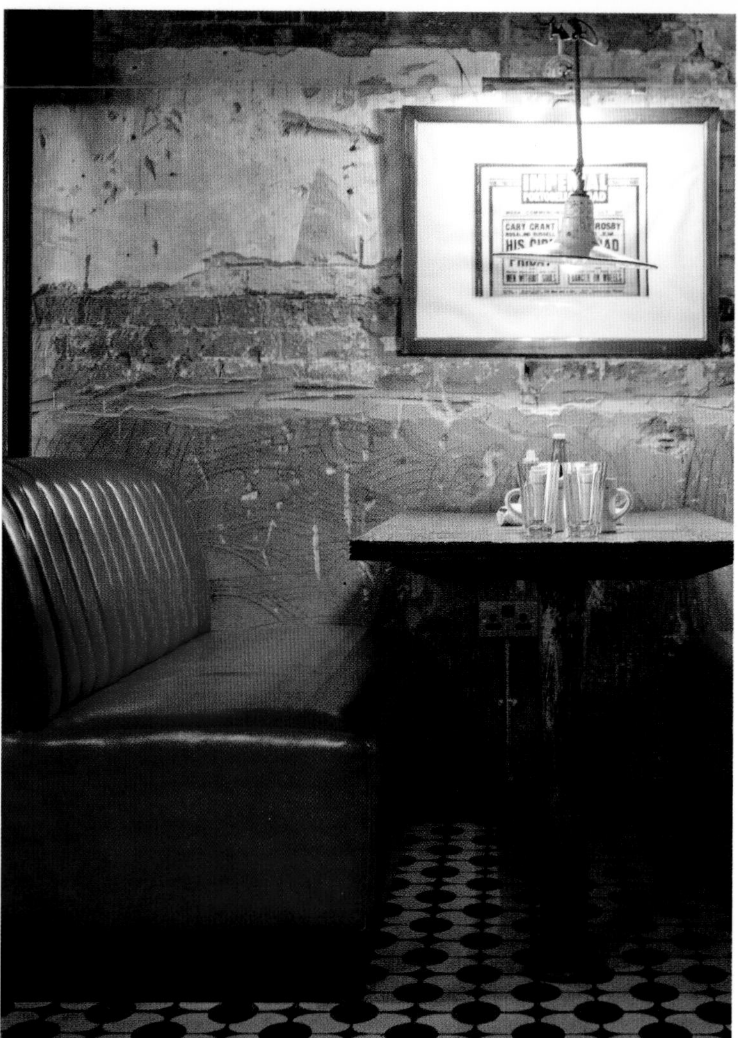

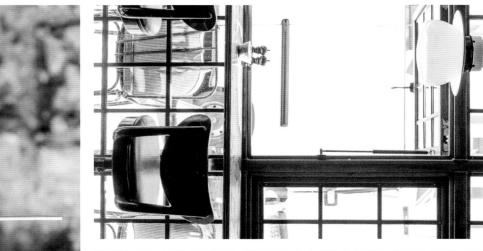

ELECTRIC DINER

191 PORTOBELLO ROAD

NOTTING HILL – LONDON, W11 2ED

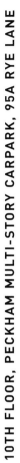

PLACE TO BE

131

FRANK'S CAFÉ

10TH FLOOR, PECKHAM MULTI-STORY CARPARK, 95A RYE LANE

PECKHAM – LONDON, SE15 4ST

MEANTIME BEER
2.25 1/2 4.50 pint
London Lager - Yakima Red
London Pale Ale - Fest Bier
Breton Cidre 4.20 330ml Btl.
Cocktails
Negroni 5
Aperol Spritz 6
Dark & Stormy 6
Amaretto Sour 6.50

FRANK'S CAFÉ

10TH FLOOR, PECKHAM MULTI-STORY CARPARK, 95A RYE LANE
PECKHAM – LONDON, SE15 4ST

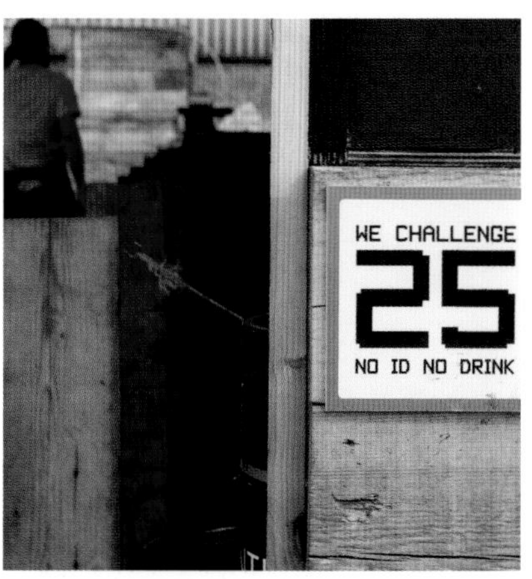

Every summer, at the top of a bleakly urban multi-storey car park in deepest Peckham, one of London's coolest, most unusual bars pops up, courtesy of Frank Boxer – brother to Brunswick House's Jackson and grandson of famous food writer Arabella. With its red tarpaulin roof covers, wooden benches and makeshift bar slamming out short, sippable cocktails, there's a scintillatingly rough and ready, Berlin-meets-Ibiza-in-the-early-years energy to this place. Zeitgeisty installations from the Bold Tendancies contemporary art collective and unbeatable views of the London skyline are the setting for long, lively evenings fuelled by Aperol spritzes and 'Dark and Stormy's'. These days, food scenesters are as visible here as the art crowd, drawn to the kitchen's simple, seasonal plates of sardines and harissa, grilled sweetcorn with smoked paprika or wonderfully rustic hummus with toasted sourdough.

35 SPITAL SQUARE

SPITALFIELDS – LONDON, E1 6DY

GALVIN LA CHAPELLE & CAFÉ A VIN

GALVIN LA CHAPELLE & CAFÉ A VIN

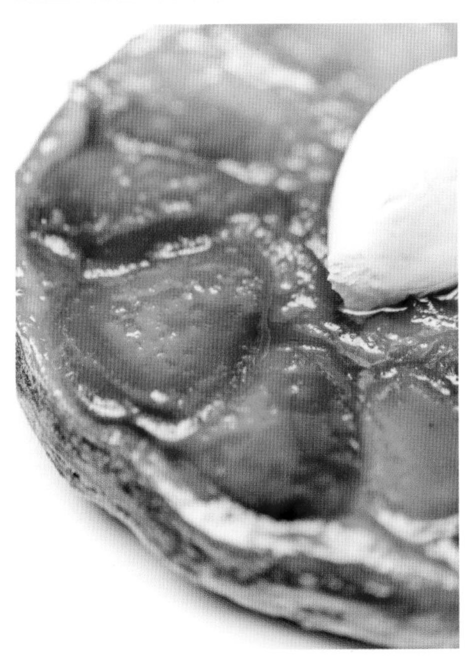

'It was the site really; it was this building that made us want to open another restaurant,' says Jeff Galvin, who, along with brother Chris, fell in love with the Grade II-listed chapel of a former girls' school in Spitalfields. 'It even looked beautiful derelict, with no roof. It was a challenge – in a building with so much history you want to do it justice.' The Francophile chef brothers have since won a Michelin star for the grand, sumptuous fine-dining restaurant La Chapelle, where you can eat their signature Bresse pigeon tagine, rich with aubergine purée and harissa sauce. They have also gained wide acclaim for the attached Café a Vin, which showcases natural wines and simple, delicious French fare like the crave-inducing tarte flambée.

PLACE TO BE
139

HAWKSMOOR

157A COMMERCIAL STREET

SPITALFIELDS – LONDON, E1 6BJ

HAWKSMOOR

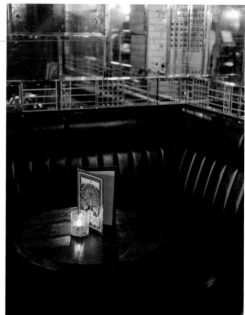

It's true that there were steakhouses in London before Hawksmoor, but none of them quite captured the capital's frenzied inner carnivore quite like this meaty restaurant group. The flagship site in Spitalfields was where Londoners fell back in love with British beef – after an adulterous interlude with some of its Argentinian and Japanese relations. But the founders insist that, despite travelling the world, affectionately reared rare-breed longhorn cattle from North Yorkshire is the tastiest in the world, and the capital has absolutely agreed with them. Properly aged, flame grilled and offered up in its various cuts – bone-in prime rib, porterhouse, T-bone – by weight and according to availability, the steak here is unparalleled. Pour over the bone-marrow gravy and dunk in your triple-cooked chips, while you sink a palate-provoking 'Full-fat Old Fashioned', made with butter-infused bourbon. Then go for a run.

PLACE TO BE
141

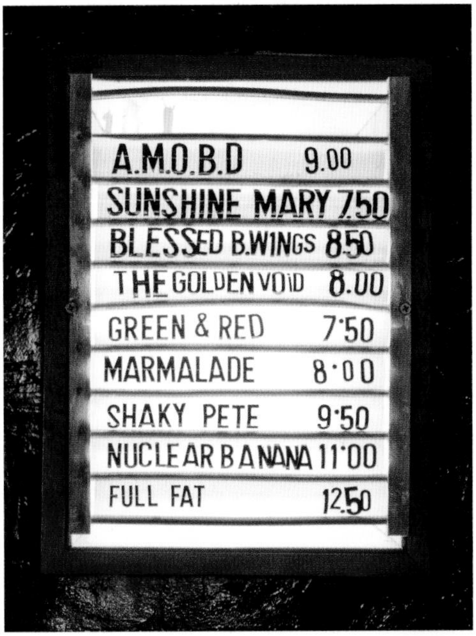

A.M.O.B.D 9.00
SUNSHINE MARY 7.50
BLESSED B.WINGS 8.50
THE GOLDEN VOID 8.00
GREEN & RED 7.50
MARMALADE 8.00
SHAKY PETE 9.50
NUCLEAR BANANA 11.00
FULL FAT 12.50

157A COMMERCIAL STREET

SPITALFIELDS – LONDON, E1 6BJ

HAWKSMOOR

PLACE TO BE
143

HONEST BURGERS

UNIT 12, BRIXTON VILLAGE

BRIXTON – LONDON, SW9 8PR

GREAT BRITISH

Free range chicken
CHICKEN
Chicken, lettuce, tomato & mustard mayonnaise £8.5
BEEF
Beef, red onion relish, & lettuce £7.50
CHEESE
Beef, Red Onion Relish & Lettuce with Mature Cheddar, Red Leicester or Stilton £8
HONEST £9
Beef, Red Onion Relish, Smoked Bacon, mature Cheddar, house pickles & lettuce.
HAND PICKED
House Chips with rosemary salt
House dressed Salad
Beetroot & Apple Coleslaw
All £2.5
SPECIALS
Beef, Bacon, Applewood Smoked Cheddar, Chipotle BBQ, Lettuce & Griddled Courgette £10.50

HONEST BURGERS

The burgers created at the original, miniature Honest Burgers site in Brixton Village covered market created such a frenzy amidst the capital's carnivores, and such a long queue, that the owners took pity and opened another site in Soho, and then Camden. Forget American burgers though, these patties are proud to be British, and are made with meat sourced from the excellent Ginger Pig butcher and rare-breed farmer, whose pigs, cattle and sheep are reared on the North Yorkshire Moors. All burgers come in a glazed bun with rosemary-tossed home-made fries, and specials include creative, produce-driven delights like the beef and black pudding burger with apple tempura, tarragon and caper mayonnaise, and baby leaf lettuce.

LA FROMAGERIE

2-6 MOXON STREET

MARYLEBONE – LONDON, W1U 4EW

LA FROMAGERIE

While she now has two of London's best-loved cheese shops and two highly regarded specialist cheese books to her name, Patricia Michelson's quest to bring brilliant farmhouse cheeses to the capital started on a whim. Returning from a Méribel ski trip clutching a whole wheel of Beaufort Chalet d'Alpage, she duly sold it from her garden shed and then a Camden market stall, eventually opening the first shop in Highbury in 1992. The delightful Marylebone site launched in 2002, and both shops now house on-site maturing cellars, where cheeses are delivered direct from artisan producers and matured by in-house affinage (specialist cheese maturers), as well as impressive, wonderfully pungent walk-in cheese rooms, delis and cafes. Cheeses span goat's, buffalo, sheep and cow's milk, and include creations like the lovely soft Portuguese sheep's milk cheese Azeitão, which is made with artichoke thistle rennet and has a sharp, sweet earthiness to it.

LA FROMAGERIE

2-6 MOXON STREET

MARYLEBONE – LONDON, W1U 4EW

MARTELL'S

LES TROIS GARÇONS

1 CLUB ROW

SHOREDITCH – LONDON, E1 6JX

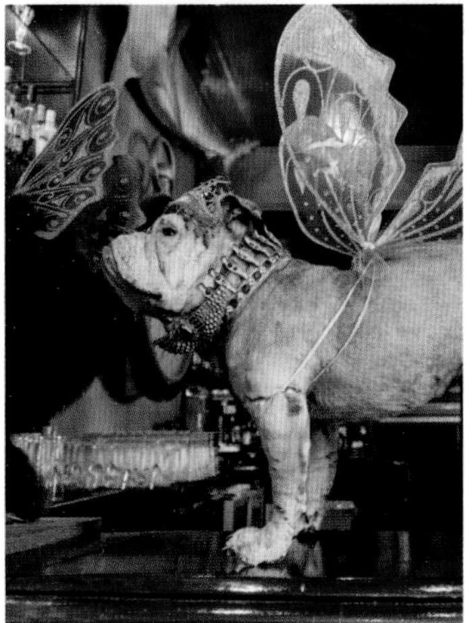

LES TROIS GARÇONS

A good decade before Shoreditch would become a swarming ground for art, fashion and food-scenesters, Hassan Abdullah, Michel Lasserre and Stefan Karlson – three successful interior designers – had the foresight to buy this glorious building on the Bethnal Green Road and make it their home. In 2000, these 'trois garçons' opened the ground floor up as one of London's most memorable and eccentric dining rooms, while keeping the upstairs for their living quarters and the cellar stocked with fine wine. A meal here is taken in the company of a veritable Noah's Ark of antique taxidermy, including Boris the bulldog (a Victorian-era fighting dog donned in a pair of fairy wings) and George the giraffe (who was one of the first of his species at London Zoo), plus a rare blue Murano chandelier from the 1920s. A visual feast indeed, but also a culinary one, as chef Michael Chan melds classic French haute cuisine with Asian and New World accents to produce memorable, harmonious dishes like crayfish and sweetbread spring roll with black sesame-dressed bean sprouts. Front-of-house guru Fabien Babanini is a wine enthusiast who loves nothing more than exploring regions and grapes with you as you eat, making for a beautifully bacchanalian experience.

18
MONOCLE
18
THE MONOCLE CAFE

18 CHILTERN STREET

MARYLEBONE – LONDON, W1U 7QA

MONOCLE CAFÉ

THE
MONOCLE
CAFE

MONOCLE 24

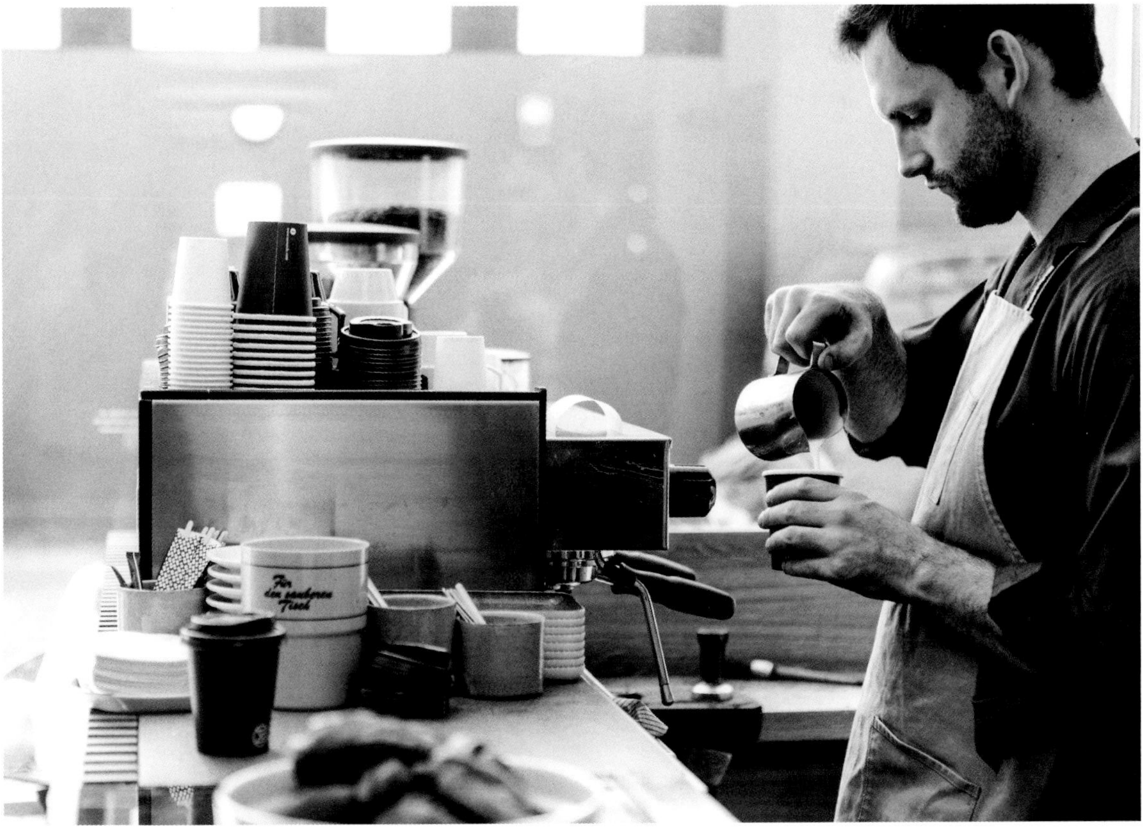

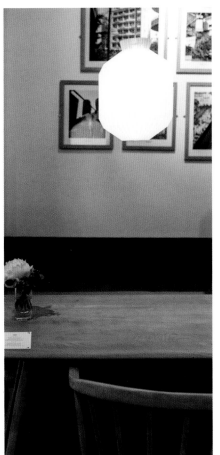

MONOCLE CAFÉ

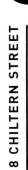

In 2013, international affairs and design-bible *Monocle* followed its Tokyo cafe opening with one in London, near to its headquarters, on Chiltern Street in Marylebone. To create their 'dream cafe', the team behind the magazine led by publisher and *Wallpaper** founder Tyler Brûlé, called on their multiple industry-leading connections, resulting in a unique and modish coffee shop. As you'd expect from a global design journal, the interior is captivating, if somewhat understated – a sleek confluence of clean lines and beautiful natural materials like red oak, which has been used to create bold Japanese-style screens. Coffee is roasted daily, and comes courtesy of the New Zealand-Australian team Allpress Espresso, while food is fresh and hearty cafe fare: wholesome Bircher mueslis, seasonal salads and cheese toasties. The cakes here are even worth putting down a copy of *Monocle* for; created by former Le Gavroche pastry chef Masayuki Hara's Lanka bakery, they include fresh macarons, green tea roll cake and strawberry gateau.

itt
-Cue-

PECIALS

MOKED OX CHEEK
ONEMARROW TRENCHER

MOKED PIG'S HEAD
N W/ 'NDUJA

EXTRAS

SMOKED CHIPOTLE WINGS
LOADED SKINS
CRUMBED PIG'S CHEEK

TAKEAWAY

PULLED P
HOUSE SA

1 NEWBURGH

SOHO – LONDON, WIF 7RB

PITT CUE CO.

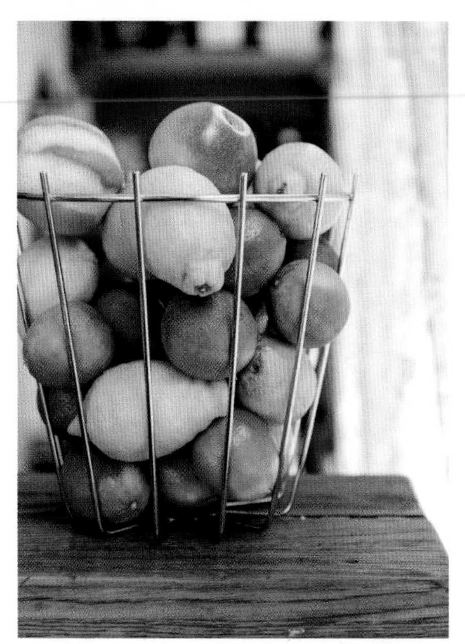

DISTILLED AND BOTTLED IN KENTUCKY
HEAVEN HILL
CUSTOM MADE MASH
Old Style Bourbon
Kentucky Straight Bourbon Whiskey
Distilled and Bottled by

WHATEVER
PITT CUE Co.

1 NEWBURGH
SOHO – LONDON, W1F 7RB

PITT CUE CO.

London knew its street-food revolution meant business when vendors began swapping pavements for bricks-and-mortar sites in prime restaurant territory. What started as a food truck on the South Bank, delighting with its seriously smoking southern American-inspired barbecue, moved into a tiny, 24-cover premises in Soho a year after it began peddling its slow-cooked brisket, pulled pork and proper home-made baked beans. Led by a crack team, including lauded head chef Tom Adams and bourbon expert Jamie Berger, this basement barbecue joint has a bar upstairs where you wait (there are no reservations) in the good company of picklebacks – bourbon shots chased by pickle juice. When your table is ready, descend into the cosy dining room and fill your belly with smoky, meaty treats from the ever-changing menu. Watch out for the 'burnt ends mash': potato purée mixed with the smoky, charred ends of the brisket.

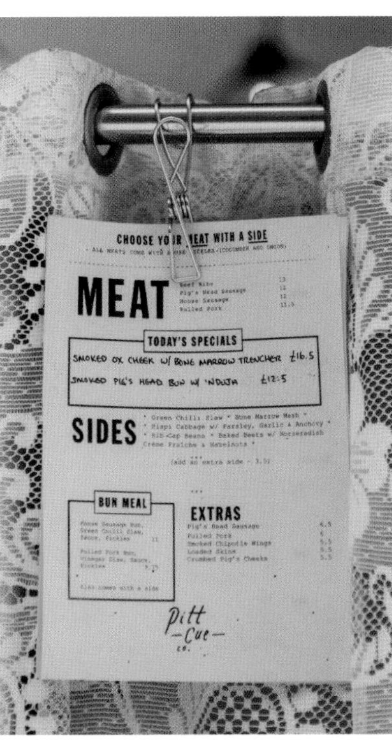

PITT CUE CO.

PIZZ

56 SHOREDITCH HIGH STREET

SHOREDITCH – LONDON, E1 6JJ

PIZZA EAST

PIZZA EAST

Eating pizza in London got a whole lot sexier when the brains behind the Soho House group launched this flagship site in the ground floor of Shoreditch's sprawling Tea building. Inside, a dimly lit industrial-chic interior is the setting for friends to come together over wood-fired pizzas. Melding classic Neapolitan simplicity with more progressive ideas, pizzas span everything from the classic margherita to the more elaborate pork belly with tomato, mozzarella and mushroom, or the veal meatballs with prosciutto and cream. This is very much a modern pizzeria that makes a point of using carefully sourced, seasonal ingredients, and there's a take-away counter where guests can pick-up cavolo nero, radicchio and fennel bulbs for their own kitchen.

PIZZA EAST

56 SHOREDITCH HIGH STREET

SHOREDITCH – LONDON, E1 6JJ

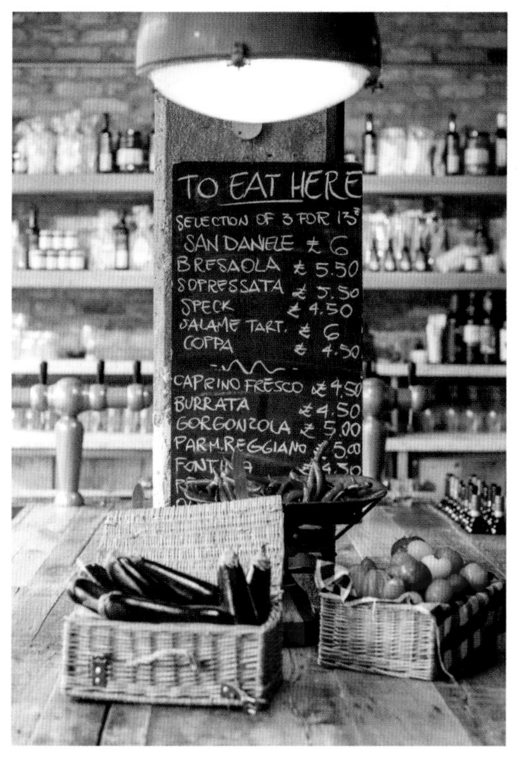

Extra Vergine
Torinesi

PLACE TO BE
167

POLPO

41 BEAK STREET

SOHO – LONDON, WIF 9SB

POLPO

This was the first solo restaurant from Russell Norman – the man credited with starting a 'fun dining' revolution in London just as recession took hold – and it's still one of the capital's coolest places to eat. Tucked away in Soho, and based on Norman's interpretation of the booze-soaked bàcari of Venice, it's a place to come with friends and lovers to share the small, addictive plates of Venetian food. Slurp on Campari house cocktails while you nibble arancini, other cicheti dishes and the famous pizzetta bianca, then get stuck into main dishes like the linguine vongole, calf's liver with onion and sage, and fennel, almond and curly endive salad.

POLPO

41 BEAK STREET

SOHO – LONDON, W1F 9SB

BREAKFAST
- Eggs - Any Style on Toast £4.50
- Granola, Poached Fruit & Yoghurt 4.00
- Toast & Jam 2.00
Caravan Coffee
Rare Teas - Olive Leaf
2.50 - Oolong
- Green

ROCHELLE CANTEEN

ROCHELLE SCHOOL, ARNOLD CIRCUS

SHOREDITCH – LONDON, E2 7ES

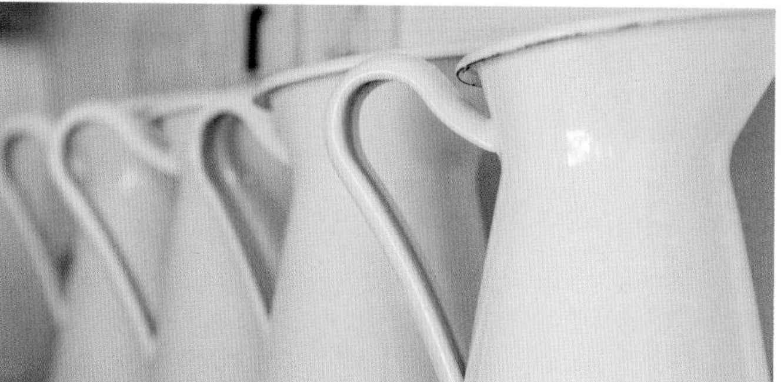

ROCHELLE CANTEEN

Ring the bell to be let into this hidden feasting spot, set in a converted school bike shed on Shoreditch's Arnold Circus in the Boundary Estate – London's first, and arguably most handsome, council housing development, which is now home to bijou shops and eateries. Margot Henderson (wife of Fergus) can be found serving up confident, unapologetically rustic breakfast, lunch and dinner dishes from the open kitchen during the week. A slow-braised cuttlefish sings of the Mediterranean and comforts the palate: rich and unctuous with sweet fennel and melting tomatoes. Sliced sirloin is ruby red and served on dripping fried bread with creamy, cutting horseradish. Cabbage comes a vital bright green, crunchy and slathered in butter. This is personal, generous cooking, by and for people that love eating.

ROCHELLE CANTEEN

ROCHELLE SCHOOL, ARNOLD CIRCUS

SHOREDITCH – LONDON, E2 7ES

ROKA

37 CHARLOTTE STREET

FITZROVIA – LONDON, W1T 1RR

ROKA

Tell any food-loving Londoner you've got a table at Roka and the reaction is usually the same. There'll be a flicker of jealous rage across their face (unless of course, you're taking them) and then a wide, dreamy-eyed smile as they recall the last time they ate there. Inspired by six years of cooking in Tokyo, chef Rainer Becker, along with restaurateur Arjun Waney, took the informal Japanese dining concept of izakaya – casual eateries with sharing plates – and brought it to London with the hit launch of Zuma in Knightsbridge in 2002. Roka followed on Charlotte Street in 2004, with an emphasis on robatayaki – dishes from the robata grill. Sit at the smooth, knotted wooden counter, sip a shochu cocktail and watch the chefs at work while you hoover up the beautiful poached king crab leg with avocado, gems of punchy tosazu jelly and wasabi roe.

37 CHARLOTTE STREET

FITZROVIA – LONDON, W1T 1RR

ROKA

PLACE TO BE

179

20 MOUNT STREET

MAYFAIR – LONDON, WIK 2HE

SCOTT'S

SCOTT'S

First an oyster warehouse founded in 1851, and then a restaurant in its current Mayfair location since 1968, Scott's has long been a haunt of the rich and influential, and it's still got it. Famed for its seafood, and for being the place Ian Fleming discovered the dry martini 'shaken, not stirred', this is a proper grown-up London restaurant. It's a place best reserved for blow-outs (because who wants fruits de mer without some very good white wine?), but it's open all day, so you can just slink in for a quick bite at the twinkly oyster bar, if that's how you do things. In the summer, the restaurant's terrace is one of the hottest tickets in town, and there are few things better than spending a few hours out here mining a lobster – alone or in good company – with a bottomless carafe of white Burgundy.

20 MOUNT STREET

MAYFAIR – LONDON, W1K 2HE

SCOTT'S

61
SPUNTINO
4

SPUNTINO

61 RUPERT STREET

SOHO – LONDON, WID 7PW

61 RUPERT STREET
SOHO – LONDON, W1D 7PW

SPUNTINO

When the queue subsides and you bag your seat at the shining zinc counter of this diner-cum-dive bar in the heart of Soho's porn district, one of the tattooed staff will plant down a perfectly battered enamel cup of freshly popped popcorn. Then it's a case of choosing your poison. Try the 'Cynar Gin Fizz' – a lively, quenching blend of gin, lemon juice, Prosecco and Cynar – before you settle into the menu. Small plates are a signature of Russell Norman – the restaurateur behind this and the hugely successful Polpo group – and the food is Italian with a strong New York accent. Pimped-up junk food like the rich, runny truffled egg toast, beef and marrow sliders and stuffed fried olives are crave-inducing, but it would be a shame not to try some of head chef Rachel O Sullivan's more demure dishes, like quail with romesco or the puntarelle, fennel and anchovy salad.

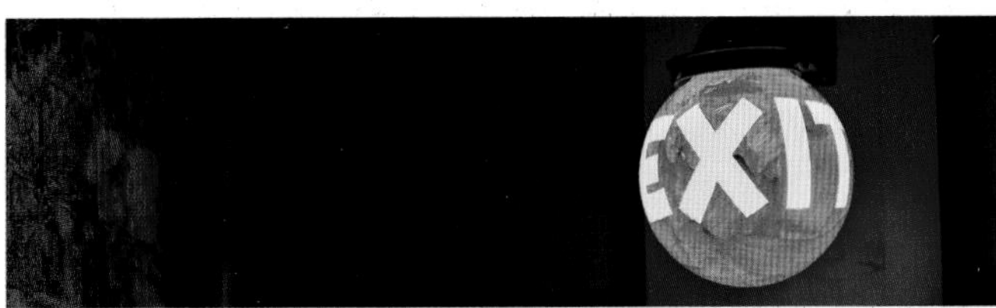

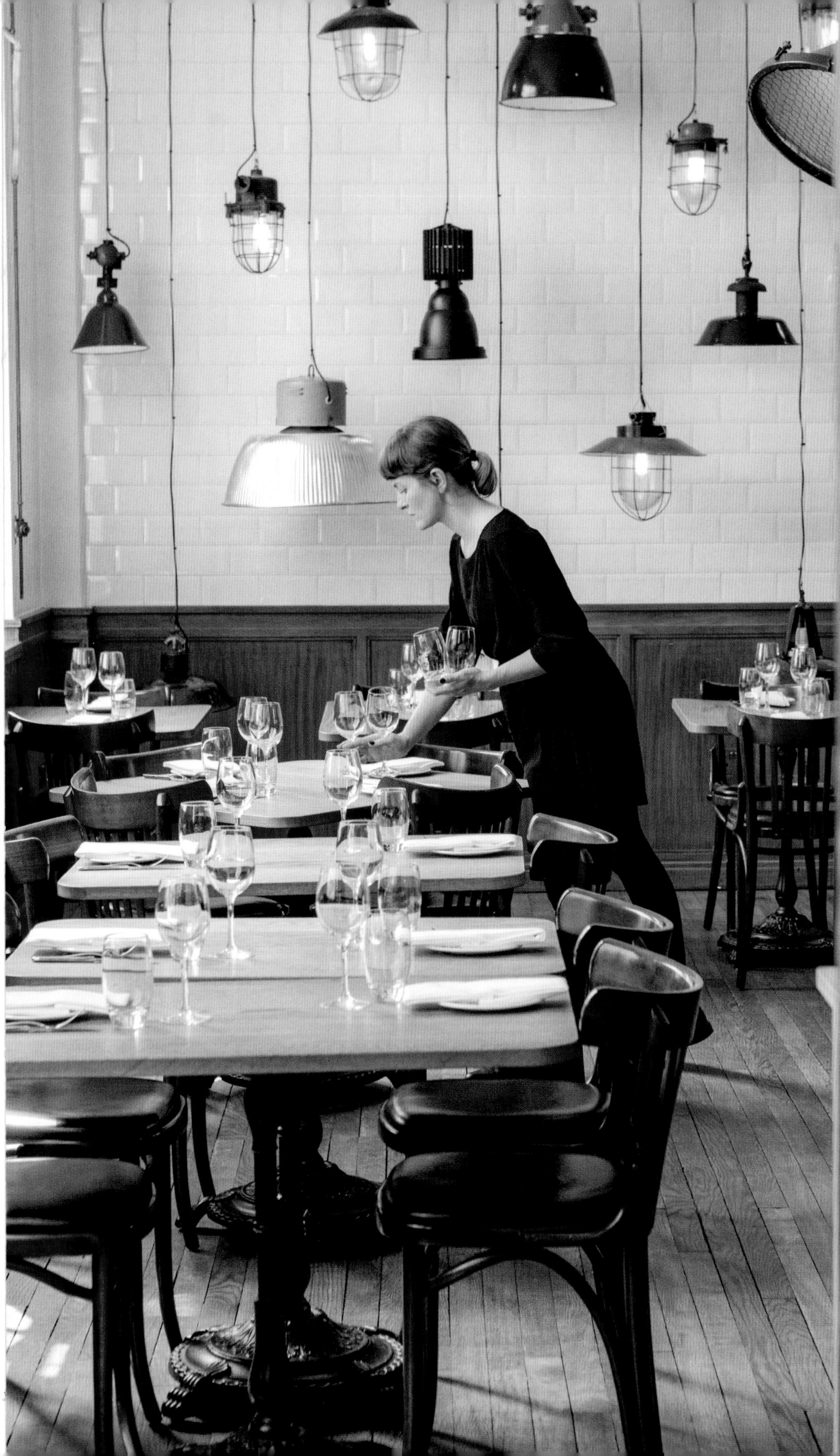

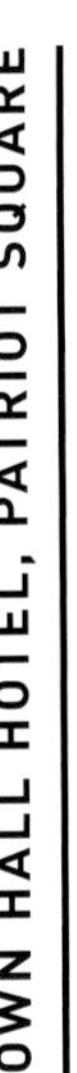

VIAJANTE & THE CORNER ROOM

VIOLET
• Egg, Paprika, Mayo, Herb, Olive + Feta Sandwich 6.00
• Comte + Our Chutney Sandwich 5.00
or Toastie 5.50
• Cheddar + Onion Toastie 5.50
• Buffalo Mozzarella, Ham + Rosemary Toastie 6.50
• Savoury bread pudding w. spinach, mozzarella + ham + salad 7.00
• Leek + Stanley Quiche 7.50
• Ham, Comte + Thyme Quiche 7.50
• Spring Salad
Small (side) 3.50
Large (main) 5.50
VIOLET
Americano
Hot chocolate
Filter Coffee
French press
Iced Coffee
Babyccino
Glass of Milk
Amalfi lemonade
English Apple juice
Sparkling water
TEA
Earl Grey
Dragonwell green
Oolong
Buckwheat
Peppermint
Lemon Verbena
small pot 3.50
large pot 6.00
Jasmine pearls
Pu'erh
small pot 4.00
large pot 7.00
WHOOPIE PIE
Edible Selby
VIOLET
CARROT CAKE WITH CREAM CHEESE ICING
VIOLET
CHOCOLATE MARSHMALLOW WHOOPIE PIE
STRAWBERRY CUPCAKE

47 WILTON WAY

HACKNEY – LONDON, E8 3ED

VIOLET

VIOLET

'It's the artisanal — it's about making something by hand in the best possible way, with the best possible ingredients, because it tastes better, and because it's just nice. It's nice to have this connection with people along the way — to build relationships with the people that give you your organic eggs or your milk. When I first opened the bakery, people wouldn't deliver all the way out to where I am on Wilton Way in Hackney, but now there are so many different businesses it makes sense for suppliers to do so, which is great for everyone. The name comes from my childhood obsession with these delicious-smelling flowers. The violet is a flower you can't cultivate: if you try, it loses its scent, and that speaks to the whole thing too.' *Claire Ptak*

VIOLET

47 WILTON WAY

HACKNEY – LONDON, E8 3ED

PIZZA
choose from
fresh from the oven
£11.50 EACH
TOMATO, BASIL and MOZZARELLA
SALAMI, TOMATO, CHILLI and MOZZARELLA
MUSHROOM, CARAMELISED GOATS CHEESE
AUBERGINE, COURGETTE, SUNDRIED TOMATO and ARTICHOKE
PARMA HAM, TOMATO and ROCKET
CHICKEN, GREEN CHILLI, PESTO, RED ONION, TOMATO and MOZZARELLA
TAKE OUT TWO FOR £15.00

YORK & ALBANY

127-129 PARKWAY

CAMDEN – LONDON, NW1 7PS

DonJulio
TEQUILA REPOSADO
Crème de Cassis
Curaçao Orange
Liqueur de Rose
Menthe Blanche
Curaçao Bleu
Manzana Verde
Curaçao Orange

C
D

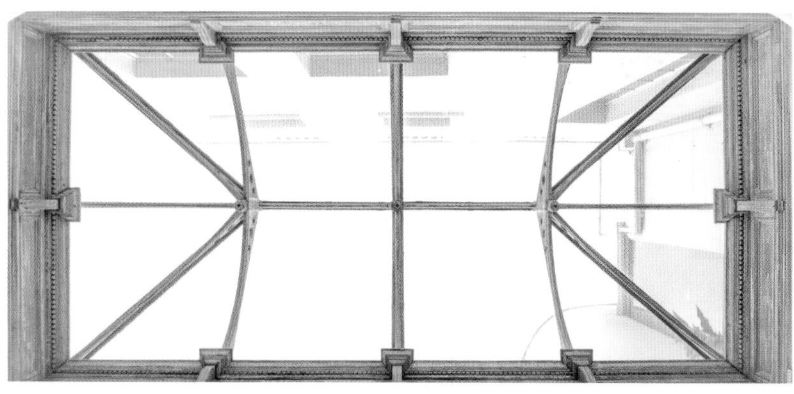

YORK & ALBANY

We all know Gordon Ramsay isn't one to do things by halves, and this ambitious venture in Regent's Park shows us why his restaurant portfolio is still holding steady on the fickle London scene. At once a bar, gastronomic restaurant, boutique hotel, gourmet deli and wood-fired-pizza takeaway counter, this elegant Georgian townhouse is a cordial place to find yourself if you're in need of any kind of refreshment. In the restaurant, long-time Ramsay protégé and head chef Kim Woodward has created a harmonious menu of seasonal, proudly British dishes; you'll find lamb sweetbreads flirting with bedfellows mint and broad bean in the summer, or whole, roasted plaice cosying up to white asparagus, monk's beard and a melting pat of shallot and herb butter.

WORLD FOOD
199

barraf

54 FRITH STREET

SOHO – LONDON, WID 4SL

BARRAFINA

Fire
escape
keep
clear

WORLD FOOD
205

BOCCA DI LUPO

12 ARCHER STREET

SOHO — LONDON, W1D 7BB

Gelato Cupcakes
Bitter chocolate & Hazelnut gelato
Pistachio & Hazelnut Gelato
Bitter chocolate & Espresso Gelato

BOCCA DI LUPO
SUNDAY SPECIALS

FLAVOURS
BONET
CHOCOLATE & SESAME
CRÈME CARAMEL
ESPRESSO
FRESH MINT STRACCIATELLA
HAZELNUT
PISTACHIO
RICOTTA AND SOUR CHERRY
BITTER CHOCOLATE
BLOOD ORANGE
KIWI, GIN & ELDERFLOWER
COCONUT
LEMON
PASSION FRUIT
RASPBERRY
RHUBARB SORBET
COFFEE & TEA
ESPRESSO
MACCHIATO
CAPPUCCINO
LATTE
AMERICANO
TEAS
AFFOGATO (WITH HAZELNUT GELATO)
CAFFE ALLO ZABAIONE (WITH BEATEN EGG YOLK)
CAFFE ALLA NOCCIOLA (WITH EGG YOLK & HAZELNUT)
BICERIN (CHOCOLATE, ESPRESSO & CREAM)
HOT CHOCOLATE, GELATO & CREAM
NEW!
THE GELUPO PIADINA
HOT, FOLDED ITALIAN
FLATBREAD SANDWICHES
DELICIOUS ITALIAN STREET FOOD

BOCCA DI LUPO

Jacob Kenedy's sleek small-plates Italian was one of the first to herald a culinary reinvigoration of this part of Soho – leading the way for a new wave of restaurants that swapped waiter-fawning formality for a laid-back style that let the food do the talking. It's since become a firm favourite, thanks to Kenedy's obsessive knowledge of the country's regional cuisine. The seasonal menu features ever-changing versions of raw and cured alongside fried and grilled ingredients, plus home-made breads, pastas and sausages. A fennel salad is piqued by deep, savoury mullet bottarga, fried sage leaves are stuffed with melting anchovy and the classic Tuscan salad panzanella is served with crispy grilled quail, while tagliatelle comes simply dressed with butter, girolles and parmesan. Over the road, sister-venture Gelupo serves up some of the city's best gelato and sorbet, all made by Italian chefs on the premises. Try the fresh mint and chocolate chip or the intense, refreshing blood-orange sorbet.

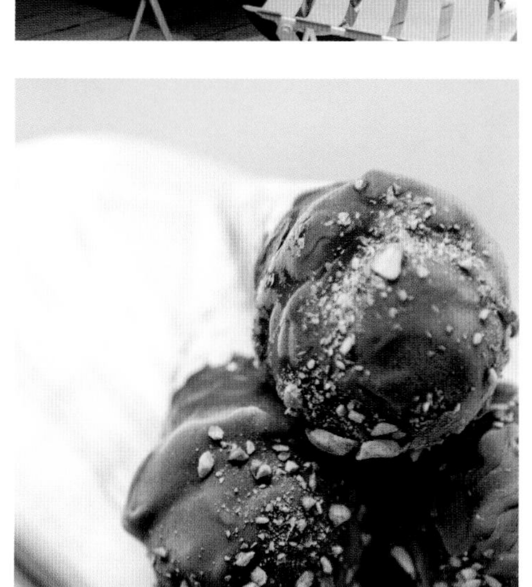

NASSERI

BRIXTON VILLAGE & MARKET ROW

ATLANTIC ROAD

BRIXTON – LONDON, SW9 8PS

BRIXTON VILLAGE & MARKET ROW

These two historic covered markets in Brixton were almost knocked down for development a few years ago, but thankfully the space was opened up to small businesses at cheap rents, and a whole host of small, idiosyncratic food start-ups launched. Now both markets are buzzing with quirky, affordable restaurants and, increasingly, chefs of calibre like Salon's Nicholas Balfe are choosing to open here. What's brilliant is that — for the time being at least — all this operates alongside the wet fishmongers, butchers and grocery shops, and cool kids rub along with locals buying their weekly shop as they have done for decades. You can eat your way around the world here — slurping Beijing noodles from Mama Lan, scoffing Neapolitan pizza from Franco Manca or eating cross-Caribbean fare from Fish, Wings & Tings — but don't neglect to investigate some of the resident traders too: Nour Cash & Carry is an Aladdin's cave of diverse ingredients, and Market Row Wines sells some fabulous bottles from small growers.

BRIXTON VILLAGE & MARKET ROW

ATLANTIC ROAD

BRIXTON – LONDON, SW9 8PS

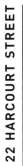

22 HARCOURT STREET

MARYLEBONE – LONDON, W1H 4HH

DININGS

DININGS

Getting a seat at this tiny townhouse Japanese in Marylebone can be tricky, and – at just 28 covers – it needs to turn tables, but once you taste the flavours coming out of the former Nobu chef Masaki Sugisaki's kitchen, you'll understand why Londoners are clamouring to get in. The food is Japanese tapas: small sharing dishes that combine Japanese and modern European cuisine to exceptional effect. Tiny bites of home-made potato crisps, topped with silky Scottish salmon and chilli miso or fatty toro tuna and wasabi mayo, are just a hint of what's to come on the extensive menu. Don't miss the sparkling sea bass ceviche with fresh truffle and ponzu jelly, and watch out for seasonal specials, like the tempura asparagus with miso.

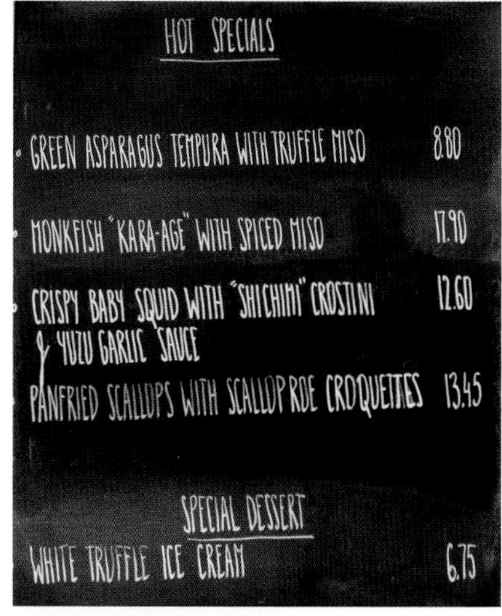

HOT SPECIALS
GREEN ASPARAGUS TEMPURA WITH TRUFFLE MISO 8.80
MONKFISH "KARA-AGE" WITH SPICED MISO 17.90
CRISPY BABY SQUID WITH "SHICHIMI" CROSTINI
& YUZU GARLIC SAUCE 12.60
PANFRIED SCALLOPS WITH SCALLOP ROE CROQUETTES 13.45
SPECIAL DESSERT
WHITE TRUFFLE ICE CREAM 6.75

WORLD FOOD
215

DININGS

22 HARCOURT STREET
MARYLEBONE – LONDON, W1H 4HH

20
HOXTON
SQUARE
भरुचा एंड सन्स प्रिंटर्स, १२ मरीन लाईनस

7 BOUNDARY STREET

SHOREDITCH – LONDON, E2 7JE

DISHOOM

DISHOOM

The eccentric, eclectic spirit of Mumbai's crumbling Irani eateries is alive and well in this corner of Shoreditch, thanks to Kavi and Shamil Thakrar, the cousins who brought their take on the Indian city's Zoroastrian cafes to London. While its spectacular interior is a visual love letter to the fading art deco grandeur of the originals, chef Naved Nasir's menus celebrate the broader cuisine of Mumbai – from its irresistible street snacks and the famous dishes of Chowpatty Beach to the Parsi specialities of the cafes. Vada pau, a souped-up version of the ubiquitous Mumbai chip butty, is a must-try: spiced, deep-fried potato patties topped with crispy batter and green chutney inside a soft white bread roll. It is best washed down with an East India gimlet: a perky tincture of Bombay Sapphire, lime and bitters that evokes the long, hazy nights of the colonial decadence of the Bombay era.

7 BOUNDARY STREET

SHOREDITCH – LONDON, E2 7JE

DISHOOM

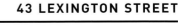

FERNANDEZ & WELLS

43 LEXINGTON STREET

SOHO – LONDON, W1F 9AL

ALL OF OUR
HARCUTERIE & CHEESES
ARE AVAILABLE
FOR TAKEAWAY
SEAFOOD
SMOKED ANCHOVY FILLETS 9'50
SMOKED BABY MACKEREL 9'50
BOQUERONES 9'50

CECINA DE LEON 5.50
CHORIZO 5.50
JESUS DU PAYS BASQUE 5.50
FINNOCCHIONA | LOMBO 5.50
PANCETTA ARROTOLATA 5.50

ESPRESSO
MACCHIATO
PICCOLO
LATTE
HOT CHOCOLATE 2.80
AFFOGATO 2.90
FRESH MINT TEA
GAZPACHO

SYNESSO

FERNANDEZ & WELLS

43 LEXINGTON STREET
SOHO — LONDON, W1F 9AL

There are few places you can absorb the hungry, lively buzz of lunchtime Soho more acutely than in Fernandez & Wells' original food and wine bar on Lexington Street. Here, amidst the hanging hams, the rather lovely oak counter becomes a mound of ciabatta-based sandwiches, filled with well-combined, carefully sourced ingredients that tell of this small cafe group's farmers'-market ethos. Favourites include the grilled chorizo with roasted red pepper, rocket and olive oil or the made-to-order 36-month-cured jamón Ibérico de bellota with tomato — considered to be one of the best sandwiches in London. Cakes and cheeses are also done well here, but it's best to finish off your lunch with a Portuguese custard tart and single-estate-bean espresso from its Beak Street cafe just around the corner.

THE GARRISON FILM
FAMILY PRESENTS
FOUR WEDDINGS &
A FUNERAL
BRIDGET JONES DIARY
SUNDAY 7·30PM 19 & 26TH MAY

99-101 BERMONDSEY STREET

BERMONDSEY – LONDON, SE1 3XB

GARRISON (THE)

THE GARRISON

Bermondsey's transformation from industrial backwater to uber-cool gourmet heartland (see also Maltby Street Market, Zucca and José) has developed along with this much-loved pub/restaurant, which opened in 2003. The hospitality visionaries behind it, Adam White and Clive Watson, met as hip young bartenders, and have a flair for creating special, well-designed spaces – having also launched Village East down the road and The Riding House Café in Fitzrovia. The venue's exposed brick and whitewashed wood-clad walls give an airy ambience, while its vintage treasures and curiosities – including a taxidermied antelope – lend a wry eccentricity. Food is modern British, so you can expect plates of pork-cheek fritters with butternut squash purée and salsa verde for lunch, or pan-roasted sea bass with red chicory, runner beans and red-wine sauce for dinner. Brunches have always been a strength here – you can break fast with a generous plate of smoked haddock kedgeree and an organic, fair-trade, London-roasted coffee.

GARRISON (THE)

99-101 BERMONDSEY STREET

BERMONDSEY – LONDON, SE1 3XB

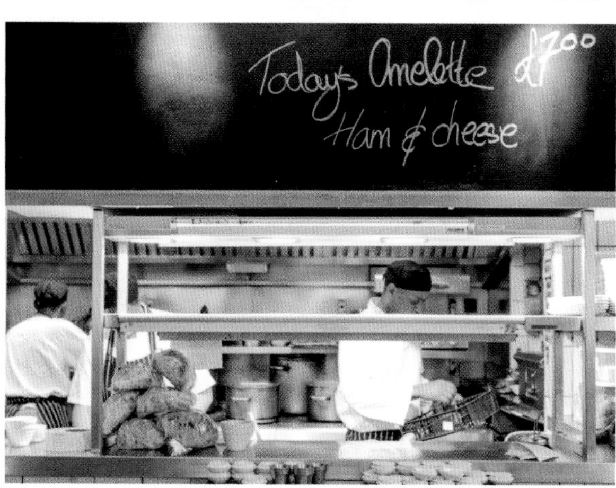

SMOKE

HANSEN &

FOUNDED 1923

3-5 SHELFORD PLACE

STOKE NEWINGTON – LONDON, N16 9HS

HANSEN & LYDERSEN

HANSEN &

Aalesund

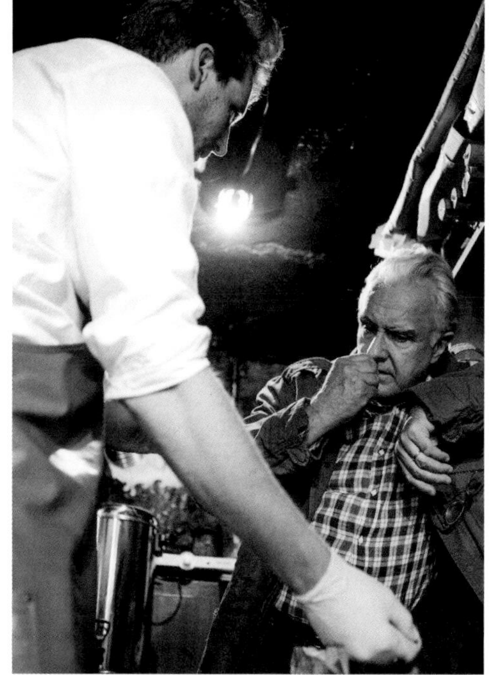

HANSEN & LYDERSEN

This smokehouse in Stoke Newington has a backstory that takes in four generations of Norwegian craft. Ole Hansen uses the old brick chimney of a former printing works as a kiln, following a smoking method developed by his great-grandfather, Lyder-Nilsen Lydersen – a fishmonger and salmon fisherman, whose smoked salmon was famous in and around the Varanger fjord. Sourced directly from the northern Norwegian Arctic, the salmon is traditionally hand-filleted, hand-salted, hung and cold smoked in the kiln for a minimum of 10 hours using a delicate blend of juniper and beechwood. The result is an intense, memorable artisan product that's won countless plaudits, and is supplied to some top London restaurants including NOPI and Sake No Hana.

The Morocco Store
MADLEY
PROPERTY SERVICES
LET AGREED
020 7378 0644
www.madleyproperty.com
José
xanders

WORLD FOOD

233

104 BERMONDSEY STREET

BERMONDSEY – LONDON, SE1 3UB

JOSÉ

JOSẼ

'When I first came up with Josẽ – a proper tapas bar inspired by the Boqueria in Barcelona – I never imagined it would be such a success. I was thinking 25 for lunch, 40 for dinner. We do 1,400 a week, and we only have 17 stools,' says José Pizarro, the Spanish chef who's been elevating Spanish cuisine in the capital through his cooking for over a decade. His two eponymous restaurants Josẽ and Pizarro in Bermondsey have been full since opening, wooing diners with the wonders of unusual Ibérico pork cuts, battered fried lamb's brains and – much to his delight - sherry. 'My customers are young people – it's not the granny drink anymore; I see people having the whole meal with sherry. People say that they come to my restaurants and feel like they are in Spain, and that's the nicest thing anyone can say to me.'

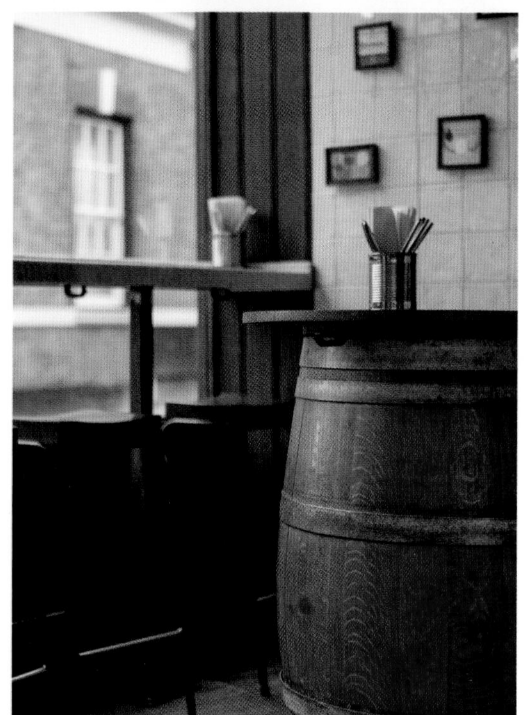

JOSĒ

104 BERMONDSEY STREET

BERMONDSEY – LONDON, SE1 3UB

FRANCIS
HARTRIDGE'S
LEBRATED RANGE
traditional
soft-drinks
ot beer
monade £2
ndelion + burdock
nger beer
TRADITION
SMOKE
HADDOC
FROM GRIMS
Supplied by
J. Bennett Jnr.
at Billingsg
Market.

WORLD FOOD
237

KINGS BOULEVARD

CAMDEN – LONDON, N1C 4AH

OUTSTANDING DELICIOUS
FREE-RANGE HAND-MADE
EGGS BREAD
From Clarence Court. Laid by Burford Brown hens.
Made free of additives by The Spence in Stoke Newington

KERB

bleecker st BURGER
MENU
Cheeseburger 500
Double Cheeseburger 790
Blue Burger 550
Veggie Burger 500
Fries

ORDER HERE
Brisket
FRIES £2.50
LASHINGS OF GINGER BEER £2.00

GOOD & PROPER
TEA Co

KERB

'KERB King's Cross is the ultimate lunchtime street-food hub in London. It's in this incongruous place – like a little oasis, existing behind the crazy transport nucleus that is Kings Cross and St Pancras on a pedestrianised, tree-lined boulevard. There's a great community of traders that vary daily, and each one is chosen because they have something amazing to offer the city. People find out about what's happening through Twitter or the website, and it's a real smorgasbord. There's everything from Japanese gyoza to Nashville buttermilk-fried chicken tacos; ox-heart burgers; or amazing hand-made ice cream with salted caramel doughnuts.'

Petra Barran

Japanese Udon
KOYA
Opening Hours
Monday - Sunday
12:00 - 15:00
17:30 - 22:30 (22:00 Sun)

KOYA

49 FRITH STREET

SOHO – LONDON, WID 4SG

KOYA

This cosy Soho spot looks unassuming, but with Japanese-born Junya Yamasaki behind the stove, it's turning out some of London's most compelling, original fare. This place is revered for its foot-rolled Sanuki udon noodles and traditional hot and cold udon dishes, and also for Yamasaki's creative specials, which apply a minimal Japanese approach to seasonal and local British produce. These are where the chef's fine art background – he studied for an MA in Paris before launching into cooking – shines through. Depending on the season, you could find a venison miso and ramson udon, or grilled, nuka-fermented sardines with pickled rhubarb; and the cold udon with hot dashi, pork and miso is a year-round winner. Yamasaki can sometimes also be found flaunting his gastronomic muscle at nearby tapas favourite Barrafina, so if you're in the area, make sure you track him down.

KOYA

49 FRITH STREET

SOHO — LONDON, W1D 4SG

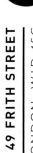

L'ANIMA

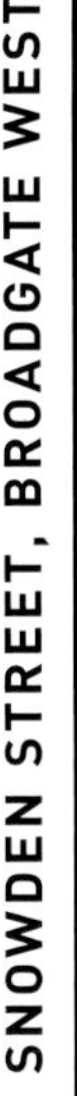

1 SNOWDEN STREET, BROADGATE WEST

CITY – LONDON, EC2A 2DQ

LIMA

LIMA

31 RATHBONE PLACE

FITZROVIA – LONDON, W1T 1JH

LIMA

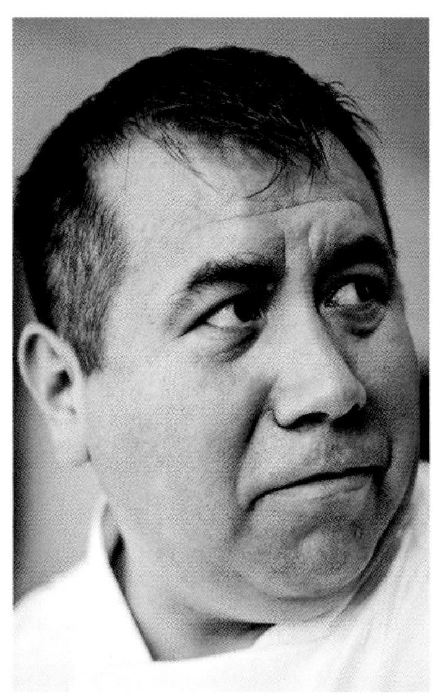

The magic of Peruvian gastronomy – with all its globally influenced twists and turns of flavour and texture – has reached London's food scene, thanks to lauded chef Virgilio Martinez. His restaurant Central, in Lima, now features on the 'World's 50 Best list', and this London cousin in Fitzrovia is turning out some of the capital's most vital and relevant food. Sit in the jewel box of a dining room and have your palate perked by unusual ingredients that speak of Peru's incredible biodiversity, artfully combined with prime indigenous British produce through the prism of Martinez's clean, contemporary cooking style. This could mean a signature ceviche of sea bream with tangy Tiger's milk (the citrussy marinade that cures the seafood), ají limo pepper, red onion and cancha corn; or pork belly with black quinoa, Peruvian yellow potato and *huacatay* (Peruvian black mint).

Push bar
PICKED

MALTBY STREET MARKET

MALTBY STREET MARKET

What started as an unofficial, esoteric offshoot of Borough Market has grown into a fully fledged food oasis and street market in its own right, housing some of the country's most exciting artisan produce and gastronomic talent. Under the old railway arches of Bermondsey's former industrial hinterland, you'll now find coffee roasters, craft brewers, artisan bakers and biodynamic-vegetable purveyors. This is the place to come for home-made, pastrami-packed reuben sandwiches at Monty's Deli, specialist imported Greek oils from Maltby & Greek, and small-grower natural wines and seasonal plates at 40 Maltby Street. Sip a smooth, site-roasted Monmouth Coffee, or a flavourful IPA from The Kernal Brewery, as you hunt down the perfect courgette flower or wild mushroom from Tayshaw greengrocer. And make sure you carry a napkin — you'll need it to wipe the custard off your chin after one of the St. John Bakery's renowned doughnuts.

MALTBY STREET MARKET

Mangal II
TAKE AWAY
AVAILABLE

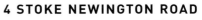

MANGAL II

4 STOKE NEWINGTON ROAD

STOKE NEWINGTON – LONDON, N16 8BH

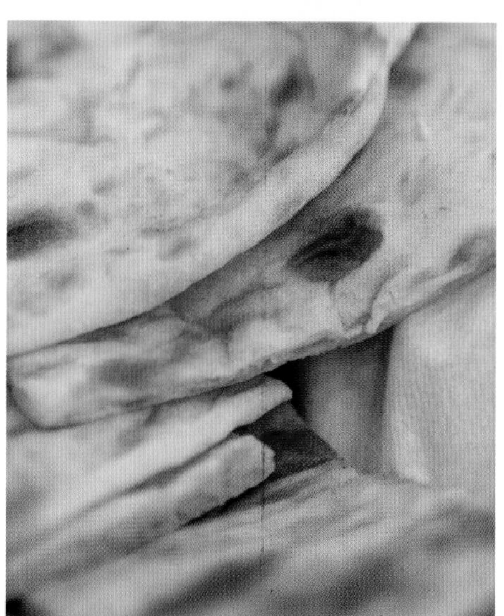

THE TEMPLE OF APOLLO

MANGAL II

The charcoal grill has latterly become the must-have toy for London's more modish kitchens, but long before the 'Josper' or the 'Big Green Egg' hit high-end chefs' wish lists, this Turkish Ocakbasi (fire pit) restaurant in Dalston was rocking the hot coals. Ali Dirik was a chef in Istanbul before he came to London in the 1980s, and this place has garnered a reputation as the best Turkish in the capital, thanks to his flair for fire. Meze dishes like silky, savoury stuffed aubergines are a delight, and the onions cooked with pomegranate juice, spices and parsley wouldn't look out of place on one of the capital's trendier gourmet menus. But it's the smoke-spilling grills that will captivate your eyes, nostrils and palate when you visit. Try the sizzling lambs' sweetbreads, with their smoky crusted outsides and juicy, lush insides, or the grilled shish kebab with yoghurt and fresh tomato sauce.

MAZI
ADT

12-14 HILLGATE STREET

NOTTING HILL – LONDON, W8 7SR

MAZI

MILDR
FOOD HYGIENE RATING
5

MILDREDS

45 LEXINGTON STREET

SOHO – LONDON, WIF 9AN

45 LEXINGTON STREET

SOHO – LONDON, W1F 9AN

MILDREDS

When best friends Diane Thomas and Jane Muir moved to London from Bristol to open Soho's only vegetarian restaurant in 1988, the word on the street was that it wouldn't last six months. But their 'hip' rather than 'hippy' approach to meat-free food struck a chord with the capital long before vegetable-based cuisine became as fashionable as it is now, and, though Thomas has sadly passed away, her legacy lives on at this buzzy restaurant. There's no moral high ground here – just fresh, wholesome, often globally influenced food and a wine list that's heavy on organic and biodynamic bottles. The daily-changing burger is a must-order; based on what comes in fresh each day (this could mean carrots and courgettes one day or beetroot and black beans the next). It is seasoned with different herbs and spices, served on an organic sourdough bun and topped with rocket and home-made basil mayo.

ROYAL GARDEN HOTEL, 2-24 KENSINGTON HIGH STREET

KENSINGTON – LONDON, W8 4PT

MIN JIANG

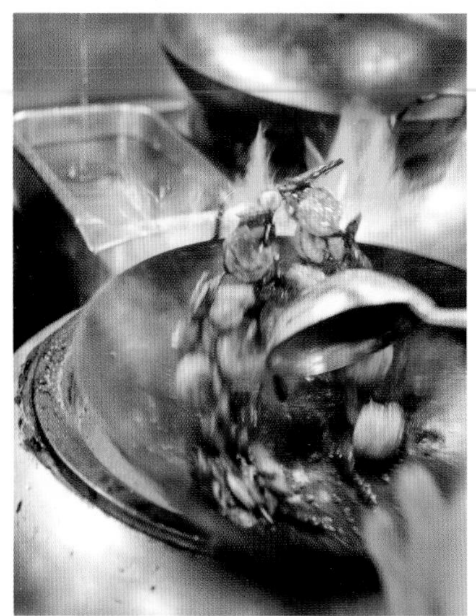

尝美膳
会聚岷

MIN JIANG

ROYAL GARDEN HOTEL, 2-24 KENSINGTON HIGH STREET
KENSINGTON – LONDON, W8 4PT

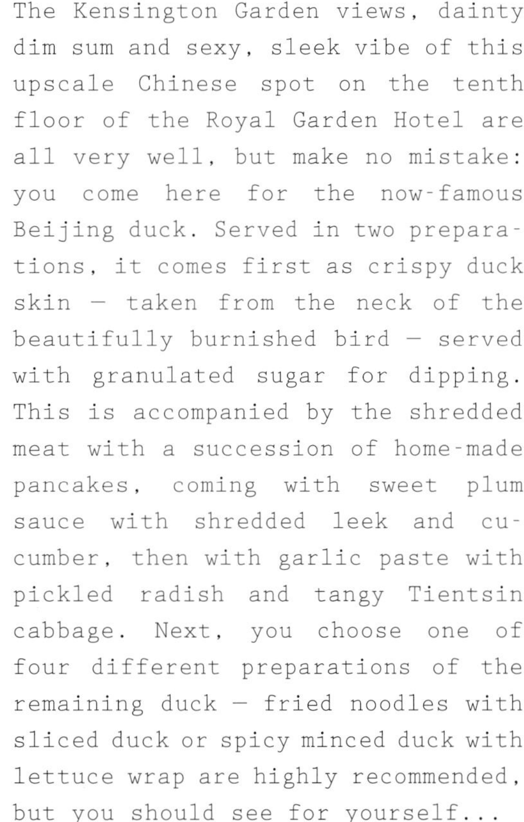

The Kensington Garden views, dainty dim sum and sexy, sleek vibe of this upscale Chinese spot on the tenth floor of the Royal Garden Hotel are all very well, but make no mistake: you come here for the now-famous Beijing duck. Served in two preparations, it comes first as crispy duck skin – taken from the neck of the beautifully burnished bird – served with granulated sugar for dipping. This is accompanied by the shredded meat with a succession of home-made pancakes, coming with sweet plum sauce with shredded leek and cucumber, then with garlic paste with pickled radish and tangy Tientsin cabbage. Next, you choose one of four different preparations of the remaining duck – fried noodles with sliced duck or spicy minced duck with lettuce wrap are highly recommended, but you should see for yourself...

MORO

34-36 EXMOUTH MARKET

CAMDEN – LONDON, EC1R 4QE

MORO

The previously overlooked offerings of the southern Mediterranean and its Moorish cuisine were given the dining platform they deserved when chef spouses Sam and Sam Clark unveiled their restaurant in Exmouth Market back in the late nineties. It's since gone on to become one of London's most influential and important dining rooms, loved for its laid-back, buzzy ambience, heartfelt open kitchen and flavour-packed plates. It has spawned various cookbooks, a little sister tapas bar and deli Morito next door and has trained up chefs like Bocca di Lupo's Jacob Kenedy. The menu changes weekly, but you could find wood-roasted chicken with slow-cooked flat beans, dukkah and seasoned yoghurt, or charcoal-grilled lamb with mechouia and harissa.

Wine Special
Soffocone di Vincigliata
Sangiovese, Tuscany, 2010
£ 15.00 glass/ £60.00 bottle

WORLD FOOD

277

OPERA TAVERN

23 CATHERINE STREET

COVENT GARDEN – LONDON, WC2B 5JS

MIND
YOUR HEAD

Berkel
1898

OPERA

OPERA TAVERN

The beast – from its nose to its tail – is king at this modern tapas restaurant in the depths of theatreland. While the pig-trotter beer taps and plates of five-year-aged jamón Ibérico de bellota give the game away, it's not just the cured stuff that's worth sniffing out. After chef director Ben Tish spent time in Spain observing the way swine is prepared there, he introduced London to such previously little-known cuts as 'secreto', the tender bit from the back of the belly, and 'presa', a shoulder cut with a sublime meat-to-fat ratio. Opera Tavern was also one of the first places to start cooking the acorn-fed Ibérico pork (he uses rare-breed British sometimes too), serving it pink to preserve its succulence and flavour – something formerly deemed unthinkable. Such cuts might be taken from the Ibérico pig, flashed on the charcoal grill and served rare, with capers and olive oil, or minced and used in the restaurant's famous pork and foie gras slider. Vegetables and fish are by no means also-rans though, and the courgette flowers stuffed with fluffy goat's cheese and drizzled with honey are a must-order.

JERUSALEM
JERUSALEM
JERUSALEM YOTAM OTTOLENGHI SAMI TAMIMI
JERUSALEM YOTAM OTTOLENGHI SAMI TAMIMI
JERUSALEM YOTAM OTTOLENGHI SAMI TAMIMI
JERUSALEM YOTAM OTTOLENGHI SAMI TAMIMI
JERUSALEM YOTAM OTTOLENGHI SAMI TAMIMI
JERUSALEM YOTAM OTTOLENGHI SAMI TAMIMI
JERUSALEM YOTAM OTTOLENGHI SAMI TAMIMI

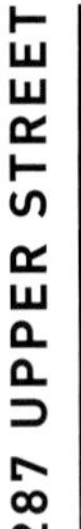

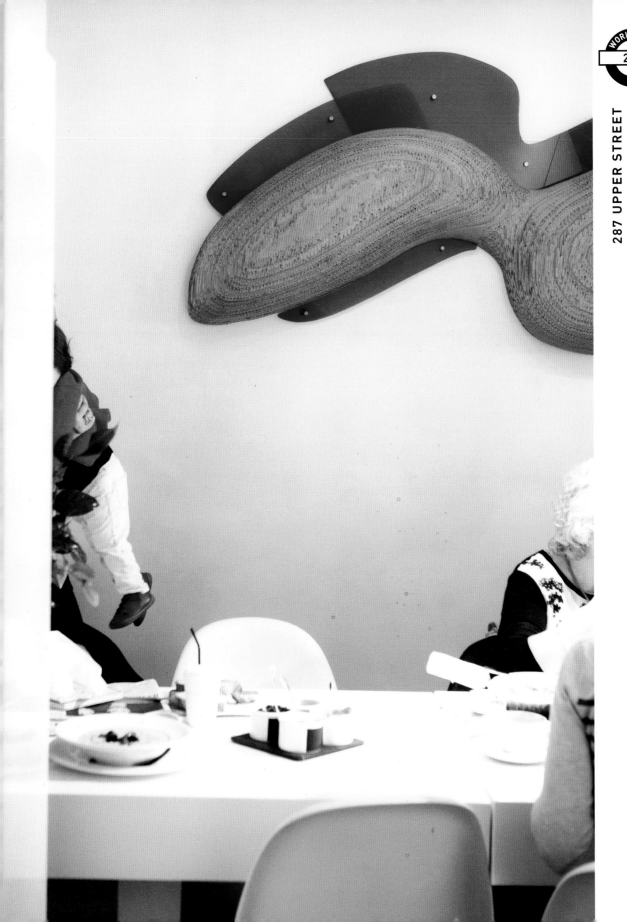

287 UPPER STREET

ISLINGTON – LONDON, N1 2TZ

OTTOLENGHI

OTTOLENGHI

Few can claim to have shaped London's palate in the way that Yotam Ottolenghi has. Before the Israeli-born chef brought his brand of vegetable-led, Middle Eastern-meets-Mediterranean-meets-Asian cuisine to the capital, words like 'tahini', 'za'atar' and 'harissa' were not a regular part of the culinary vernacular. At the Islington outpost of his deli-cum-diner, huge fluffy meringues with bright, sherbet crimson tips greet you as you enter the long, light space where those who like their vegetables dressed with delicious and disparate ingredients converge. Queue for one of the best takeaways you can get in the capital, or go and sit at one of the bright white tables and feast on rainbows of flavour: a perky slaw of rhubarb, cabbage, celery, apple and radicchio with cranberries and hazelnuts, or roasted cauliflower with cardamom yoghurt and pickled red onion.

OTTOLENGHI

287 UPPER STREET

ISLINGTON – LONDON, N1 2TZ

QUILON

41 BUCKINGHAM GATE

WESTMINSTER – LONDON, SW1E 6AF

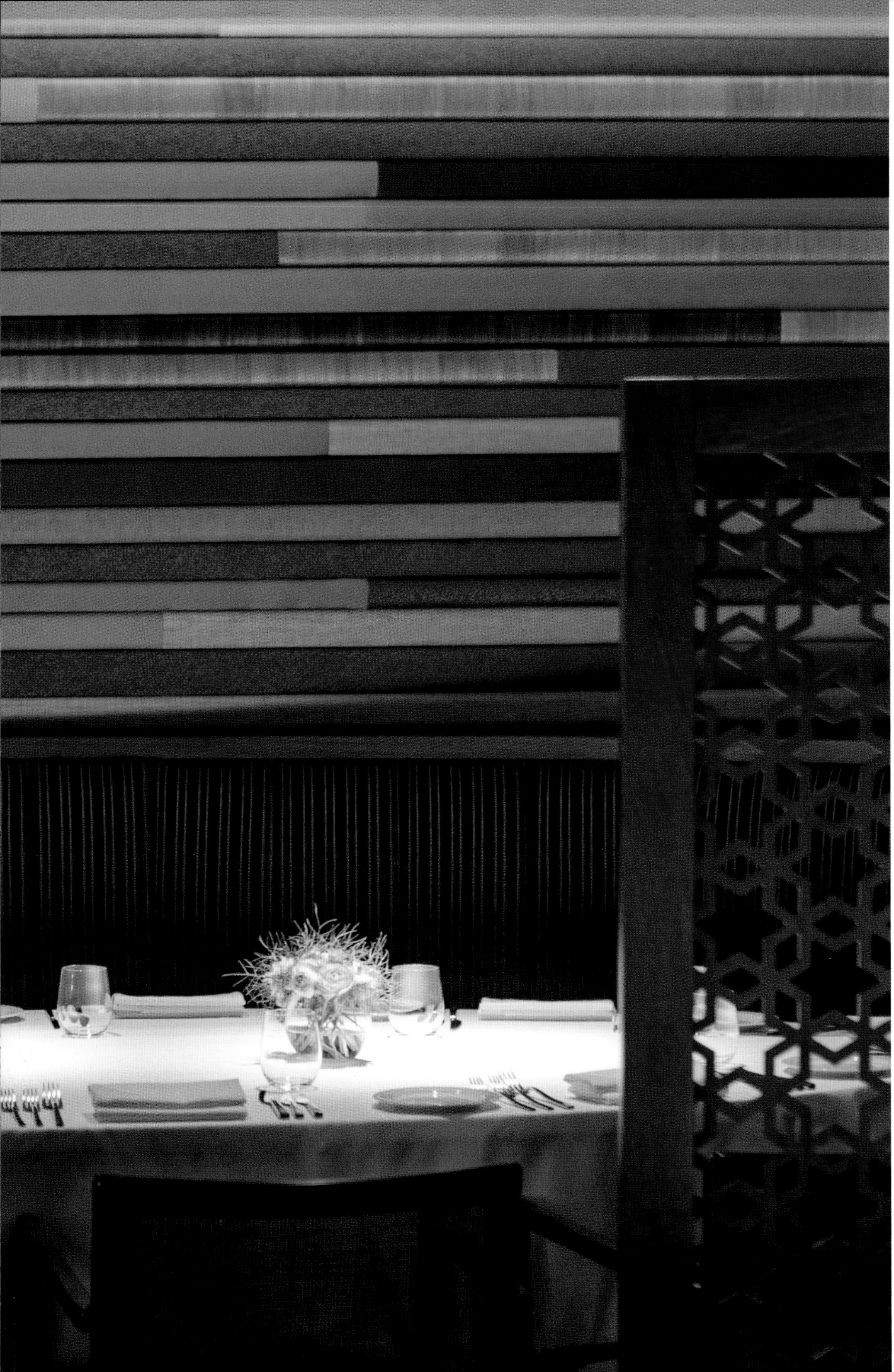

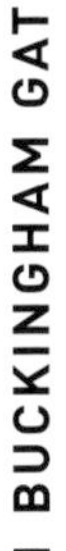

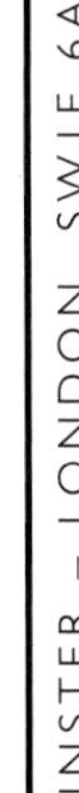

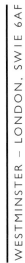

QUILON

'When we opened in 1999, we wanted to represent food from the south-west coast of India – the cuisine of Kerala, Goa, Bangalore – as this coastal food was very different from what was generally seen as Indian food in this country,' says Sriram Aylur, the chef behind Westminster's Quilon: the only south-coast Indian restaurant to hold a Michelin star. 'We wanted to do it right. That means importing five different kinds of chillies from the region.' Inside the stylish dining room, which is decked out with distinctive pieces by acclaimed artist Paresh Maity, diners taste a mixture of ethnic dishes and what Aylur calls 'progressive' dishes that meld southern coastal flavours and spicing with non-traditional ingredients, to stunning effect. Aylur enhances prime proteins like black cod, which is subtly spiced and baked, and venison fillet, which is tossed with onion, tomato, ginger and spices and cooked alongside coconut slivers.

123 BETHNAL GREEN ROAD

SHOREDITCH – LONDON, E2 7DG

WORLD FOOD

293

83-89 FIELDGATE STREET

WHITECHAPEL – LONDON, E1 1JU

TAYYABS

TAYYABS

You don't go to Tayyabs, a Pakistani cheap eat in deepest Whitechapel, for its charming service or chic decor. You go there for the tandoor – and the marinated grills and freshly baked naans the chefs fire out with it. Go in groups to try everything on the menu; book in advance to avoid queueing for hours; and try to sit upstairs, as you practically need a torch to read the menu downstairs. The lamb chops are the star here: they come sizzling, covered in a punchy marinade that will have you sucking the bones. You may not have room for dessert, but you should forget your fullness for a minute and order one of the cool, creamy house-made kulfi – pistachio and mango are the best.

UYEN LUU'S SUPPER CLUB

UYEN LUU'S SUPPER CLUB

Saigon-born, long-time Hackney resident Uyen Luu is a creative power house, counting writing, fashion, film-making and cooking among her many talents. After studying film at Central Saint Martins College and travelling all over the world, she ran her own fashion boutique in Covent Garden, which helped pay for her two-storey flat. Since 2009 she's been running her supper club from here – transforming its intimate, softly lit ground floor into London's coolest, most contemporary Vietnamese restaurant every Friday night. After a day of cooking and prep, she dons kitten heels, turns on her ample charm and plays hostess, furnishing mesmerised guests with perfectly crisp pork belly and angel's hair vermicelli while, upstairs, her mother turns out bowls of steaming, fragrant pho or big platters of tongue-tinglingly hot shredded chicken salad with daikon and banana blossom, ready to be scooped into prawn crackers and savoured. Luu's set menus showcase traditional Vietnamese dishes, and all the sweet, spicy, sour, herbal balance they entail, along with modern flourishes that speak of her global experience.

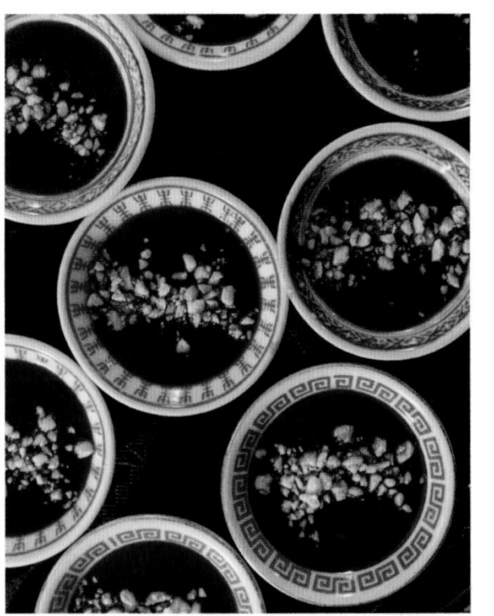

UYEN LUU'S SUPPER CLUB

YAUATCHA

15-17 BROADWICK STREET

SOHO – LONDON, W1F 0DL

丘記茶
YAUATCHA

YAUATCHA

15-17 BROADWICK STREET
SOHO – LONDON, W1F 0DL

Since it opened in 2004, people have flocked to this modern Chinese restaurant-cum-teahouse in the depths of Soho for many things: the rare blue tea selection, which is imported from Taiwan and Fujian; the little-known back bar that serves the best lychee martini you'll ever taste; and the perfect patisserie, masterminded by the Hakkasan group's executive pastry chef Graham Hornigold. In the most part, however, they come for the dim sum – and for some of the most progressive and exciting Cantonese food this city has to offer. Both the light and airy upstairs and cavernous, clubby downstairs dining rooms serve the dumpling menu, which melds traditional dishes with more modern, modish methods and flavours. The heritage dish of Shanghai siew long bun – a soup-filled dumpling usually made with pork broth – is updated with the addition of fragrant king crab, and the roasted duck and pumpkin pastry puff with pine nuts is fashioned into a beautiful miniature pumpkin. The char sui pork buns are the daintiest you'll find anywhere, while the sticky rice in lotus leaf is punctuated by addictive little cubes of smoked chicken and dried shrimp and the soft prawn and bean curd cheung fun rice noodle's crisp layer of bean curd adds structure before you reach the sweet prawn filling.

ZUCCA

184 BERMONDSEY STREET

BERMONDSEY – LONDON, SE1 3TQ

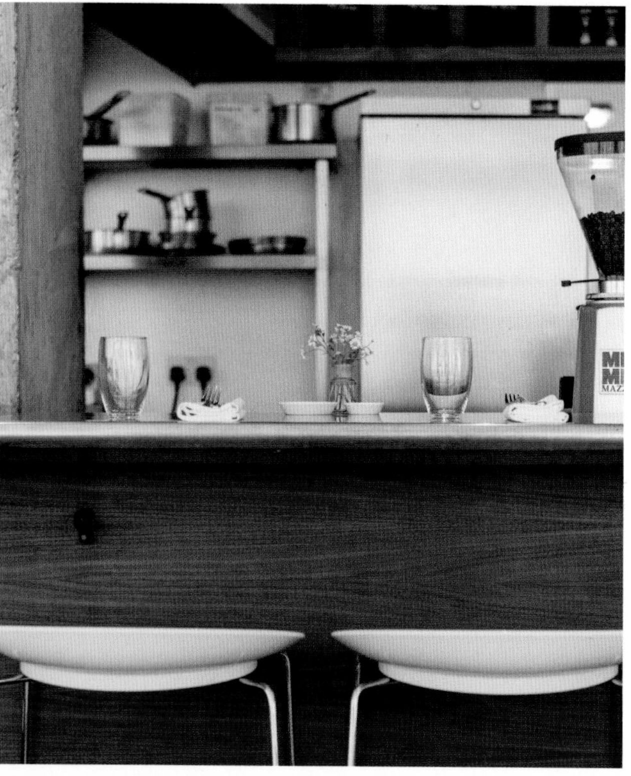

ZUCCA

'The food of Italy always struck a chord with me so much more than any other cuisine, and I wanted to create a modern Italian in London,' says Sam Harris, chef patron of this stylish, affordable restaurant, which was one of the first to turn Bermondsey Street into the dining hub it is today. 'It's so regional and so diverse I'm still learning about it now. Every time I think I'm getting to know something, I'll find something new. None of us grew up in Italy – it's our own interpretation of Italian food.' As such, Harris and his team make about 6–8 kg pasta every day and five or six types of breads twice a day, creating daily-changing menus. You might find curling octopus tentacles that have been carefully braised for five hours before being grilled and served on a silky sweet stew of aubergine, pepper and olive oil, then seasoned with mint oil and capers; or yellow polenta slick with basajo cheese and spinach. The vibe is grown-up, the decor cool Nordic, but the food has a seasonality and simplicity that smacks of the most faithful Italian.

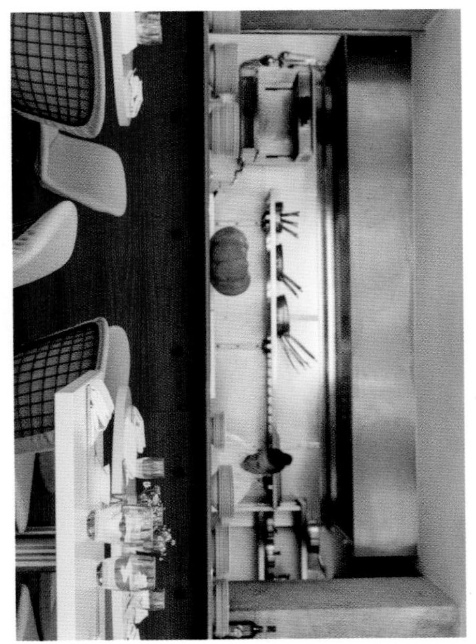

ZUCCA

184 BERMONDSEY STREET

BERMONDSEY – LONDON, SE1 3TQ

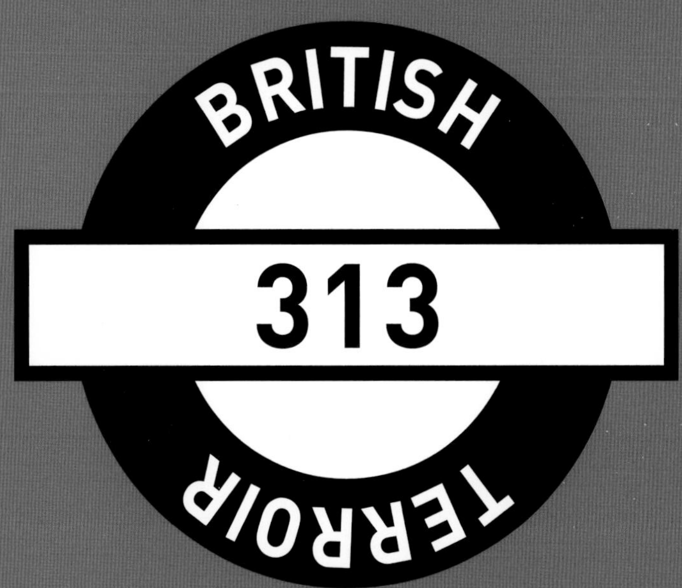
BRITISH
313
TERROIR

THE ANCHOR & HOP

36 THE CUT

SOUTHWARK – LONDON, SE1 8LP

ANCHOR & HOPE (THE)

BOMBARDIER
YOUNG'S
BITTER

CALVADOS
Šljivovica
KAHLUA
COINTREAU
Pistachios £3.50
Almonds £3.50
Olives £3.00
Crisps £1.00
Lupins .60p

THE ANCHOR & HOPE

The gutsy, unapologetic British bistro cooking at this no-reservations gastropub in Waterloo has rooted it firmly in London food legend. Spawned from the alumnus of St. John and celebrated kitchen-pub The Eagle, and itself spawning Great Queen Street in the West End, this place has been turning out affordable, seasonal plates of well-combined, simply cooked ingredients for over a decade. Attention is paid to unusual cuts – you might find a slow-braised lamb neck with dauphinois potatoes, or braised pigs cheeks alongside fennel, chorizo and mashed potato; and, while there are European inflections, dishes like potted shrimp and snail and bacon salad sing the British national anthem as you gobble them up.

RED:

11/CUVÉE DES GALETS	4.65	12.50
09/SIN SULFITO	6.00	16.50
11/FAUGÈRES (CLOS FANTINE)	7.25	19.00
11/"LA SOUTERONNE"	9.00	25.50

ROSÉ:

12/CÔTE DE PROVENCE	5.65	15.00

SWEET:

	100ml
11/MUSCAT (DOUCE PROVIDENCE)	6.00
09/JURANÇON "LA MAGENDIA"	6.75
10/MAURY ROUGE	8.00

(WHITE, RED & ROSÉ ALSO AVAILABLE IN 125ml)

49 COLUMBIA ROAD
BETHNAL GREEN – LONDON, E2 7RG

BRAWN

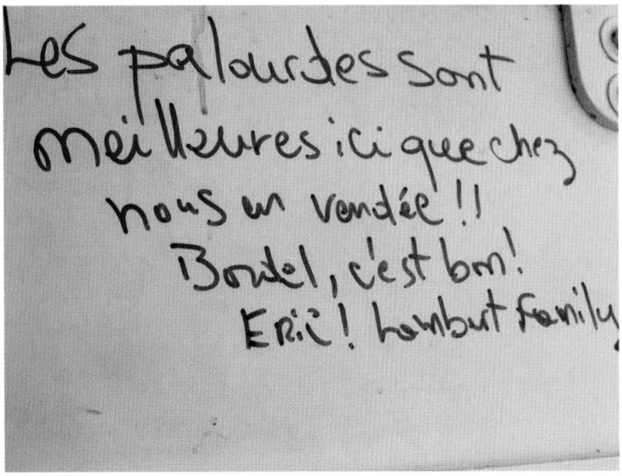

Les palourdes sont
meilleures ici quee chez
nous en vendée !!
Bordel, c'est bon!
Eric ! Lambert family

BRAWN

Provenance is the thing at this stripped-back restaurant on Columbia Road, the second venture from Oli Barker and chef Ed Wilson – the guys behind celebrated food and wine bar Terroirs in Covent Garden. Interesting, 'natural' wines, made by small producers fond of biodynamic methods and organic viniculture, draw the capital's hippest oenophiles, while its sharing plates of carefully sourced produce, cooked with Wilson's instinctive, no-nonsense approach, bait the greedy. Wilson is known for his penchant for pig (the clue's in the restaurant's name) and makes, as well as sources, some of London's best charcuterie. His Scotch eggs are made with ultra-addictive with 'nduja, the spicy, soft Calabrian sausage, while boudin noir has actual chunks of yielding pork running through it, and comes from the award-winning French producer Christian Parra.

Apple Juice
With Mixed Fruit
£3.00 bottle
Pear Juice
Apple & Rhubarb Juice
Apple & Cherry Juice
CHEGWORTH VALLEY
£ 2.95
ORGANIC ROCKET £1.00
ORGANIC SALAD LEAVES £1.00 per 100g
LAND CRESS + MUSTARD LEAVES

BROADWAY MARKET

£ 2.40
£ 2.50

CHATEAUX
GELATO

Carrot Cake
£ 2.20
Chocolate
and Vanilla Éclairs
Berries
Cheesecake Parcels
£2.80

BROADWAY MARKET

Jellied eels were first sold at this Victorian East End market in 1900, but these days its offering is a little more exotic. Alongside sharply dressed Hackney locals shopping for their fruit and veg, food obsessives swarm every Saturday for street food like the perky Vietnamese pork baguettes from Banh Mi 11, or chocolate wafer sandwich cookies from the Chez Panisse-trained baker Claire Ptak at Violet Cakes bakery stall. Permanent sites and boutique restaurants along this stretch also buzz with folk stocking up on fresh fish at sustainable fishmonger Fin & Flounder (whose seafood shack in nearby Netil Market is well worth a look), grabbing some single-origin coffee from Climpson & Sons or kicking back with some charcuterie at L'eau à la Bouche deli.

CANTON ARMS

177 SOUTH LAMBETH ROAD
STOCKWELL – LONDON, SW8 1XP

CANTON ARMS

Australian-born chef-patron Trish Hilferty lived in the Stockwell area for 20 years before she took over this south London boozer in 2010 and began turning her generous, French-inflected, modern British plates out of its kitchen. 'It had a bit of a reputation as a spit-and-sawdust Irish pub before,' says the chef, who previously cooked in the respected kitchens of Great Queen Street and The Anchor & Hope. But, far from gutting, refitting and gentrifying the pub and its dining room, Hilferty and her team have retained its original character, as well as many of its regulars — even if they now find themselves and their pints sharing the bar with government workers or younger locals sipping natural wine. Hilferty is proud of her suppliers and likes to push rare-breed meats on the daily-changing menu, with 7-hour-braised salt-marsh lamb shoulder rarely leaving her repertoire. 'It's food I like to eat — I like great big cuts — and, of course, it has to be very, very seasonal.'

177 SOUTH LAMBETH ROAD

STOCKWELL – LONDON, SW8 1XP

CANTON ARMS

IE CHELSEA SHM
Rex G
www.thechelse

CHELSEA FISHMONGER (THE)

10 CALE STREET

CHELSEA – LONDON, SW3 3QU

THE CHELSEA FISHMONGER

It's hard to believe that this thriving, white-tiled wet fishmonger in the heart of Chelsea started as a tiny stall in Surrey, but that's how Rex Goldsmith – the fish fanatic behind this place – originally set up shop. After building up a reputation supplying local restaurants with his immaculately fresh, well-sourced sea swag, business boomed, and in 2004 he took over the legendary Chelsea Fishery on Cale Street. The shop itself has 100 years of fish-trade heritage, but Goldsmith carried out a complete refit and now runs it with care for sourcing seasonal and sustainable fish and shellfish – all of which is still hand-picked from the markets in Newlyn, in Cornwall, and Billingsgate. Beautiful displays of ice-flanked fish and seafood with discernibly sparkling eyes tempt anyone a bit partial to poisson.

BRITISH 333 TERROIR

CHELSEA FISHMONGER (THE)

10 CALE STREET

CHELSEA – LONDON, SW3 3QU

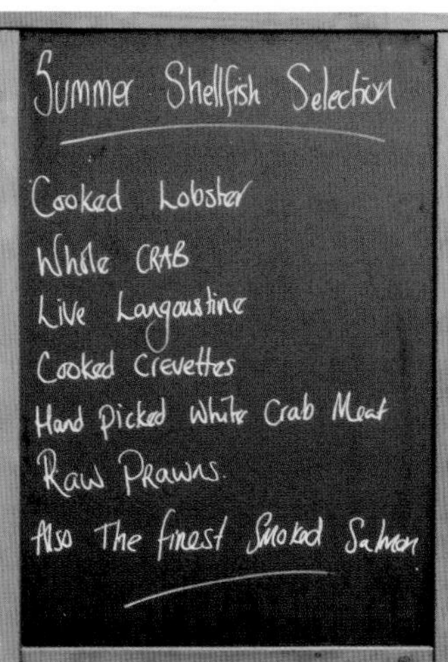

CLOVE CLUB (THE)

SHOREDITCH TOWN HALL, 380 OLD STREET

SHOREDITCH – LONDON, EC1V 9LT

BRITISH 335 TERROIR

THE CLOVE CLUB

'It's me trying to do focused new-wave British food with a bit of honesty. It's deceptively simple food in a nice, minimal room,' says Isaac McHale, one of London's most exciting young chefs. His 'Upstairs' London pop-up at the Ten Bells pub in Spitalfields was such a hit that it never popped down, and now he and right-hand men Johnny Smith and Daniel Willis, who look after front-of-house, have opened this stand-alone site in Shoreditch's Town Hall. Here, hip young things mingle with the dining cognoscenti for plates of McHale's proudly home-made rare-breed British charcuterie and cocktails in the bar, or in the stark dining room for full-blown tasting menus flaunting pristine British produce rendered through McHale's creative cooking style. His food often features unusual ingredients or parts of ingredients, like garlic scapes (the tops of the garlic plant), which come with the roasted Lincolnshire chicken and English peas. He's also one for doing progressive riffs on classic dishes – so a trout meunière might be updated using Irish pollan with green tomatoes, brown butter, elderflower vinegar sauce and dill.

DE KONINCK
BAR
THE COW
020 7221 0021
Fully
AIR CONDITIONED
spirits

89 WESTBOURNE PARK ROAD

NOTTING HILL – LONDON, W2 5QH

COW (THE)

THE COW

Tom Conran's Notting Hill Irish pub serves up big, indulgent platters of British seafood and some of the best Guinness in town. 'Eat heartily and give the house a good name' is the gastropub's mantra, and that's easy to do, either downstairs at the bar – picking your way through a whole cracked crab, whelks, winkles and Irish rock oysters with a glass of black velvet (Guinness and champagne) – or upstairs in the quirky dining room. Head chef Martin Hurrell's seasonal British menu makes for generous portions, which might include devilled lamb's kidneys on toast or smoked eel with mash, bacon and horseradish.

89 WESTBOURNE PARK ROAD

NOTTING HILL – LONDON, W2 5QH

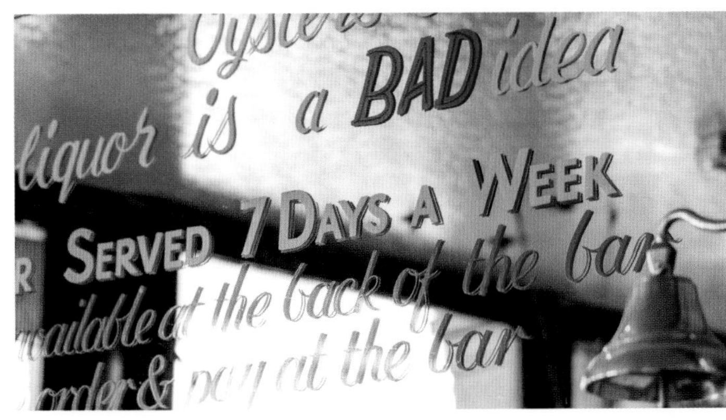

COW (THE)

BRITISH 343 TERROIR

E5 BAKEHOUSE

ARCH 395, MENTMORE TERRACE

HACKNEY – LONDON, E8 3PH

LEMON MERINGUE

ARCH 395, MENTMORE TERRACE
HACKNEY – LONDON, E8 3PH

E5 BAKEHOUSE

Looking for a change of direction from his career in renewable energy, Ben Mackinnon enrolled in a five-day course in the essentials of sourdough at The School of Artisan Food and Wine and came back a convert to the lure of natural, slow-fermentation bakery. Setting up as a nomadic baker, using a neighbourhood oven to bake his loaves, he honed his craft, eventually building his own wood-burning oven out of reclaimed materials in a derelict railway arch in Hackney; and so the E5 Bakehouse was born. Since expanding into the next-door arch, the bakery and cafe now employs what Mackinnon calls 30 'intelligent, interested, like-minded people', who deliver breads and sandwiches locally, by bicycle, to many cafes, restaurants and businesses and serve delicious lunches to those who pay a visit. Food often takes in global influences, in plates like aubergine and coconut curry with Rajasthani mango pickle, or the Spanish salmorejo (a chilled tomato and bread soup) with egg and chorizo. There are also two in-house pastry chefs, so sweet treats, like Bakewell tarts and chocolate and salted caramel tart, are as tempting as the savoury slow foods.

OPENING TIMES
Grilled Sardine Bruschetta
with Confit Garlic + Tomato £8.80
Grilled Squid + Chorizo Salad
with Rocket, Chickpeas, Parsley + Chilli Jam £14.80
Lamb Chop + Grilled Aubergines
with Mint, Lemon + Hummus £8.80
Mackerel Fillet
'Chakchouka'
Pan-fried

BRITISH
347
TERROIR

EAGLE (THE)

159 FARRINGDON ROAD
CLERKENWELL – LONDON, EC1R 3AL

MARTINI
CINZANO
CAMPARI
Havana Club
KROHN
Jose Cuervo
PLYMOUTH GIN
JIM BEAM
BOURBON
WILD TURKEY

Damm CERVESA

THE EAGLE

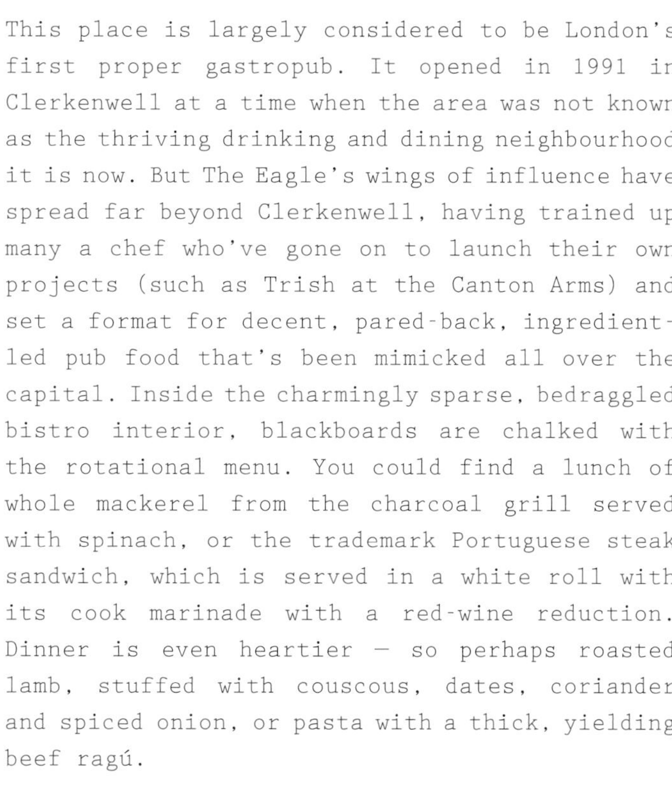

This place is largely considered to be London's first proper gastropub. It opened in 1991 in Clerkenwell at a time when the area was not known as the thriving drinking and dining neighbourhood it is now. But The Eagle's wings of influence have spread far beyond Clerkenwell, having trained up many a chef who've gone on to launch their own projects (such as Trish at the Canton Arms) and set a format for decent, pared-back, ingredient-led pub food that's been mimicked all over the capital. Inside the charmingly sparse, bedraggled bistro interior, blackboards are chalked with the rotational menu. You could find a lunch of whole mackerel from the charcoal grill served with spinach, or the trademark Portuguese steak sandwich, which is served in a white roll with its cook marinade with a red-wine reduction. Dinner is even heartier — so perhaps roasted lamb, stuffed with couscous, dates, coriander and spiced onion, or pasta with a thick, yielding beef ragú.

ELLIOT'S
TAKE
AWAY
SQUARE MILE
COFFEE

ELLIOT'S

12 STONEY STREET, BOROUGH MARKET

SOUTHWARK – LONDON, SE1 9AD

ELLIOTS RESTAURANT AND

BASED IN THE INSPIRING ENVIRONMENT THAT
IS CREATED USING THE DIVERSE INGREDIENTS A
A SIMPLE BUT MINDFUL APPROACH TO OUR COOKI
PREPARED IN SUCH A WAY AS TO SHOW THEM AT
WOOD FIRED GRILL, AND RESPECTING THE SIMP
TO FOCUS ON THE INGREDIENT BEING COOKED,

FISH

OUR FISH IS PURCHASED FROM INSHORE
FISHERMEN, OFTEN CAUGHT THE AFTERNOON
BEFORE. WE USE A BETTER + WIDER RANG
OF FISH, BUT IT ALSO ALLOWS US TO MINIMIS
WASTAGE BY CHOOSING FROM THE DAY'S CATCH,
RATHER THAN DICTATING OUR NEEDS TO
THE FISHERMEN.

FRUIT AND VEG

WE BUY PRODUCE FROM A
VARIETY OF SMALL GROWERS BASE
IN THE SOUTH OF ENGLAND, SOME OF WH
ONLY PRODUCE A SMALL SELECTION OF
INGREDIENTS THAT WE FEEL ARE THE
WE HAVE SEEN AND TASTED, AND ARE G
WITH CARE AND UNDERSTANDING.

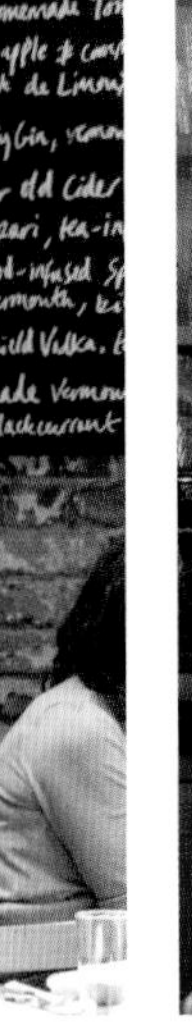

ELLIOT'S

This is the sort of restaurant you'd imagine might grow out of its surroundings in Borough Market: an organic dining microcosm which, like the market itself, relies on networks of trusted suppliers and exceptional produce to define it. Sourcing and seasonality are central here, underpinning every element of the menu, from the 40-day-aged Galloway rib-eye to the wild garlic on the garlic bread in spring, or the luscious floral honey that accompanies the goat curd on brioche – immediately transporting you to some pastoral summer meadow. If you go at lunchtime you'll also be privy to the cheeseburger, which is dreamy with melted Comte, beer braised onions and coarsely minced beef from the Ginger Pig. Exposed brickwork and simple wooden tables make for a low-key setting in which to enjoy harmonious plates like the mussels, clams, leeks and spicy 'nduja, or the Middle White pork with cabbage, pear and chervil salad. Like the culinary offering, wines are all natural, coming from small, organic or biodynamic vineyards, and the coffee is from the capital's renowned Square Mile Roasters.

69
Fin

71 BROADWAY MARKET

HACKNEY – LONDON, E8 4PH

FIN & FLOUNDER

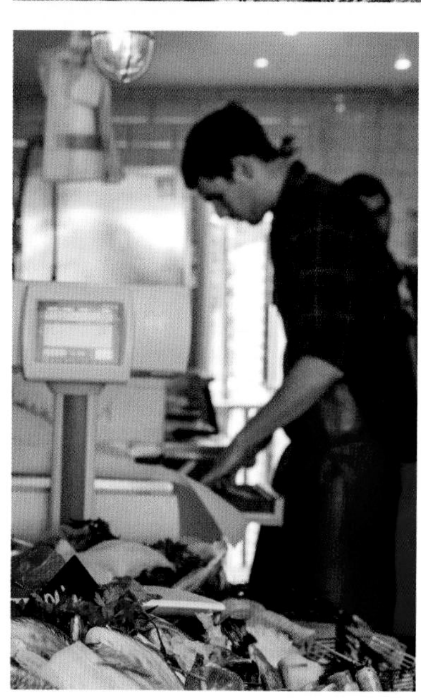

The Great British

71 BROADWAY MARKET
HACKNEY – LONDON, E8 4PH

FIN & FLOUNDER

At this wet fishmonger on Broadway Market, mounds of crushed ice shimmer with perfect specimens of local, seasonal fish from around the UK's coastline. Clams and squid vie for your attention next to whole crabs and glittering bass. The friendly staff are keen to share their knowledge and will talk you through how exactly to cook your cod's cheeks, while they fillet you a fresh mackerel or clean you some bream. Following the lead of the MSC (Marine Stewardship Council) in using sustainable approaches to provide its plentiful sea bounty, the shop has everything else you might need to conjure a fishy feast – from fresh herbs and spices to a wine selection chosen to compliment the seafood on offer.

A SOHO PUB IS UNOFFICIAL
HEADQUARTERS OF FREE FRENCH
LE GRAND VIN D'ALSACE
HUGEL
DISCLAIMER NOTICE
The management cannot accept responsibility for the Loss or Damage from any cause whatsoever to Hats, Coats, Umbrellas, or Other Articles left unattended on these premises
MESSIEURS
POUSSEZ

FRENCH HOUSE (THE)

49 DEAN STREET

SOHO – LONDON, W1D 5BG

THE FRENCH HOUSE

This legendary Dean Street drinking den opened in 1910 and has long been a favourite among Soho's bohemians, artists and food influencers – pouring its half pints (the only measure for beer here) for everyone from Lucian Freud to Dylan Thomas. A fine choice of champagnes and French wines keep the oenophiles coming back, and its tiny upstairs kitchen has a reputation for launching chefs: having been the place that first introduced London to the cooking talents of Fergus and Margot Henderson, and later lady-of-the-moment Florence Knight, who ran Polpetto here until it moved to bigger premises. These days its two floors are all about the drinking and conversation, with a no- music, television or phone policy and simple plates of charcuterie, salad and soup until 4pm.

FRENCH HOUSE (THE)

49 DEAN STREET

SOHO – LONDON, W1D 5BG

Ginger Pig
FARMER OF FRE
2
RANGE RARE BREEDS
Ginger Pig
Ginger Pig

8-10 MOXTON STREET

HACKNEY – LONDON, W1U 4EW

GINGER PIG (THE)

THE GINGER PIG

London's most respected rare-breed farmer-cum-butcher began trading its high-welfare meat products at Borough Market in the 1990s. It now has shops across London, as well as supplying some of the capital's top chefs. This East London butcher opened in 2008, and is a meat fiend's dream, stocking nose-to-tail cuts of lovingly grown, rare-breed animals – from grass-fed longhorn cattle to Tamworth and Old Spot pigs and blackface sheep. Most of what ends up changing hands here in Hackney was reared on its own farms in North Yorkshire, though the butcher does also source some carefully reared Limousin veal, poultry and charcuterie from Rungis market in Paris. This shop doubles as a deli downstairs, so make sure you snaffle out one of its legendary sausage rolls while you stock up on pies, pâtés and preserves.

GINGER PIG (THE)

8-10 MOXTON STREET

HACKNEY – LONDON, WIU 4EW

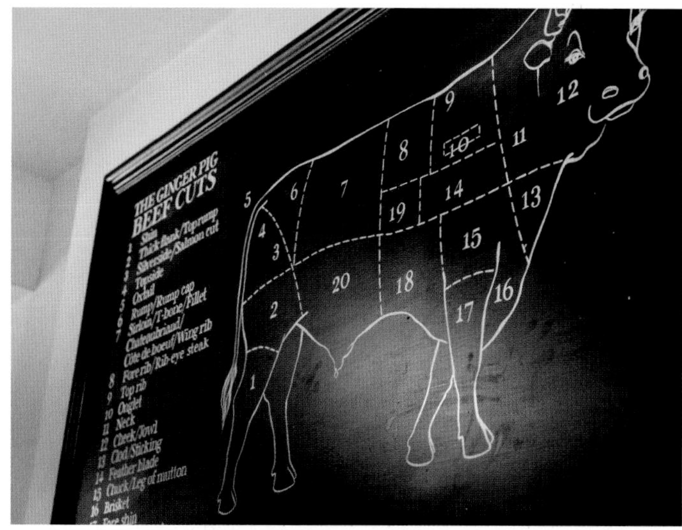

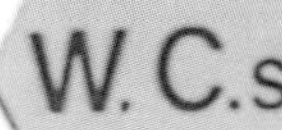

1A GOLDSMITHS ROW

HAGGERSTON – LONDON, E2 8QA

ACKNEY CITY FARM

HACKNEY CITY FARM

Goats, pigs, forest gardens and beehives might not be the first thing you'd expect to find in inner-city Hackney, but this urban-pastoral dichotomy has been delighting visitors with its rural rituals for over 20 years. As well as being a fun day trip, with the chance to get up close and personal with some furry farmyard animals, the city farm offers a wide selection of courses, which cover everything you might need to know about self-sufficiency, from edible-mushroom cultivation to keeping chickens, building your own wood stove and growing vines for city wine-making. An award-winning cafe with agriturismo menus of ingredients sourced from Kent farms and salad leaves grown, and picked by Hackney's Growing Communities, keeps visitors well nourished.

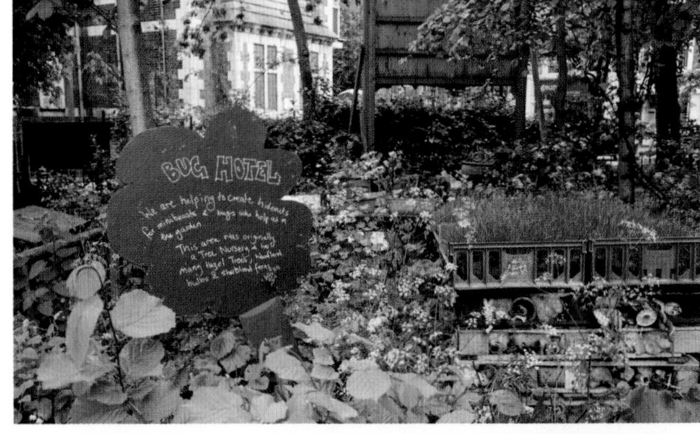

1A GOLDSMITHS ROW

HAGGERSTON – LONDON, E2 8QA

HACKNEY CITY FARM

BRITISH 371 TERROIR

3 HEREFORD ROAD

NOTTING HILL – LONDON, W2 4AB

HEREFORD ROAD

HEREFORD ROAD

'It always seemed a shame to me that there were never many British restaurants here in London. The perversity was that young people learning to cook were learning French and Italian things. So my aim with Hereford Road was to have a neighbourhood restaurant that did accessible, reasonably affordable British food, using local, seasonal produce, and the whole of the animal. There was a challenge there, in that we needed to get away from the school-dinners, meat-and-two-veg associations, and we've had to be inventive. So rather than chunking up an oxtail, as is usual, I cook it whole, braising it in a rich stock with baby carrots for a long time. We do a lot of offal: sweetbreads, tongue, liver, brains, kidneys, but I also try to balance that with a lighter touch – so lots of salad and fresh fish.' *Tom Pemberton*

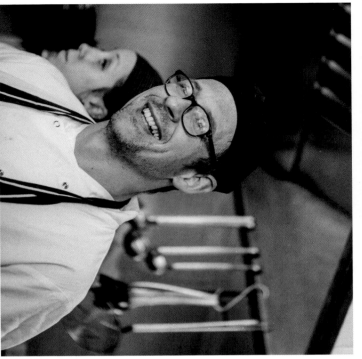

HEREFORD ROAD

3 HEREFORD ROAD

NOTTING HILL – LONDON, W2 4AB

LAUNCESTON PLACE

1A LAUNCESTON PLACE

KENSINGTON – LONDON, W8 5RL

LAUNCESTON PLACE

'I don't do surprises – the surprise should be the quality of what you eat,' says classically trained, Yorkshire-born head chef Tim Allen, who won Launceston Place its first Michelin star in 2012. At this sophisticated Kensington spot, prime British vegetables, meat and fish are treated with the utmost respect, being cooked with assured French technique and assembled into picture-perfect plates with simple, stunning elegance. The innovative vegetarian salad has become a hero dish, flaunting myriad vegetables at the peak of their freshness, each cooked sublimely and in a different way – perhaps you'll find pickled carrots or salt-baked root vegetables – combined with ice lettuce: a miraculous moisture-dappled leaf with citric acidity that dresses the salad as you eat it.

1A LAUNCESTON PLACE

KENSINGTON – LONDON, W8 5RL

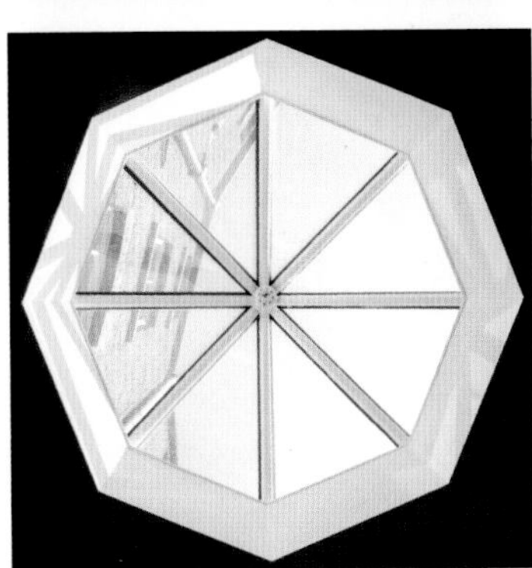

LAUNCESTON PLACE

NEAL'S YARD DAIRY
NFC
»RapidNFC
NEAL'S YARD DAIRY
farm cheese and produce
from the
BRITISH ISLES
STAWLEY

NEAL'S YARD DAIRY

17 SHORTS GARDENS

COVENT GARDEN – LONDON, WC2H 9AT

CLTHERSTONE
£27.50
CORNISH YARG
£23.05
DUCKETTS CAERPHILLY
£24.50

MEAUX
£22.15/KG
OGLESHIELD
Made by Jamie Montgomery & team, Manor Farm, North Cadbury, Somerset.
Unpasteurised
Jersey Cows
Trad. Animal Rennet
£23.85/KG

CASHEL BLUE

17 SHORTS GARDENS
COVENT GARDEN – LONDON, WC2H 9AT

NEAL'S YARD DAIRY

'When does tradition begin? It's a sort of nebulous term because every "tradition" has begun somewhere,' says Jason Hinds of Neal's Yard, the dairy and cheese monger that has been championing British cheesemaking for the past few decades through both its wholesaling and its shops in Covent Garden and Borough Market. As well as supplying well-known 'territorial' British cheeses like Colston Bassett Stilton – to which Alain Ducasse at the Dorchester has dedicated an entire trolley – it stocks unusual cheeses, made by what he calls a 'new wave' of British cheesemakers, like the raw, almost meaty, Cumbrian sheep's milk St James. 'There are people who are creating new and original cheese, and there's this pioneering spirit, which is exciting to be around. We're seeing more cheeses coming to us which are inspired by, but not 'native' to the UK.'

48 NEWMAN STREET

FITZROVIA – LONDON, W1T 1QQ

NEWMAN STREET TAVERN

Chef Peter Weeden is so scrupulous about his suppliers and so passionate about British produce – wild and otherwise – that given half the chance he'll tell you how exactly how the dayboats he uses jig-lure the squid on his menu, or why their position on Cornwall's Helford River is so special. Weeden leads a kitchen with an emphasis on tradition, so the chefs are up with the lark to bake bread, and ageing, butchery and fishmongery are all done on site. Sit on the bustling ground floor of this former pub in Fitzrovia and slurp Colchester rock oysters and natives from the raw bar, or head upstairs to the dining room proper for the à la carte menu, which might feature Middle White pork, beer and onions, or hot cockles and clams with pickled ramson. The Tavern's interesting wine list matches the menu for small, artisan producers and is the handiwork of Nigel Sutcliffe, previously of The Fat Duck.

48 NEWMAN STREET

FITZROVIA – LONDON, W1T 1QQ

NEWMAN STREET TAVERN

LD08 JXC

PIMLICO ROAD FARMERS' MARKET

ORANGE SQUARE

PIMLICO – LONDON, SW1W 8UT

NOWLE

CANVAS BAGS
Fresh from
Farmer Fridd's Farm

Cranberry Cheddar Cheese

ASPARAG

ORANGE SQUARE

PIMLICO – LONDON, SW1W 8UT

PIMLICO ROAD FARMERS' MARKET

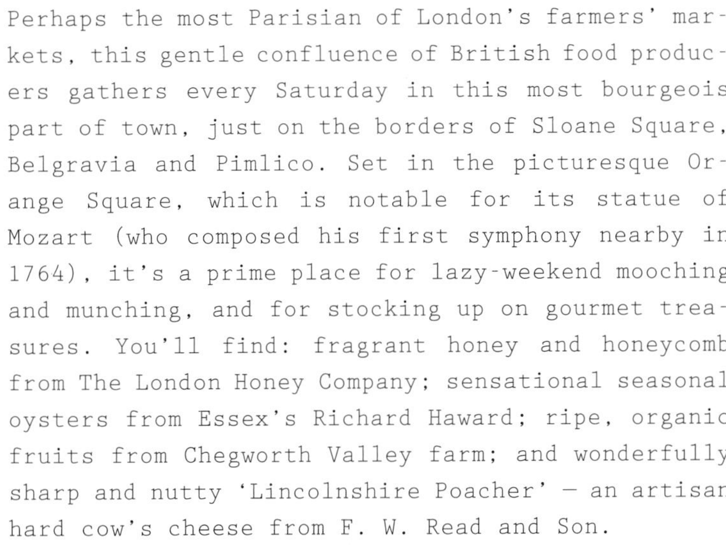

Perhaps the most Parisian of London's farmers' markets, this gentle confluence of British food producers gathers every Saturday in this most bourgeois part of town, just on the borders of Sloane Square, Belgravia and Pimlico. Set in the picturesque Orange Square, which is notable for its statue of Mozart (who composed his first symphony nearby in 1764), it's a prime place for lazy-weekend mooching and munching, and for stocking up on gourmet treasures. You'll find: fragrant honey and honeycomb from The London Honey Company; sensational seasonal oysters from Essex's Richard Haward; ripe, organic fruits from Chegworth Valley farm; and wonderfully sharp and nutty 'Lincolnshire Poacher' – an artisan hard cow's cheese from F. W. Read and Son.

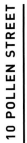

POLLEN STREET SOCIAL

10 POLLEN STREET

HANOVER SQUARE – LONDON, W1S 1NQ

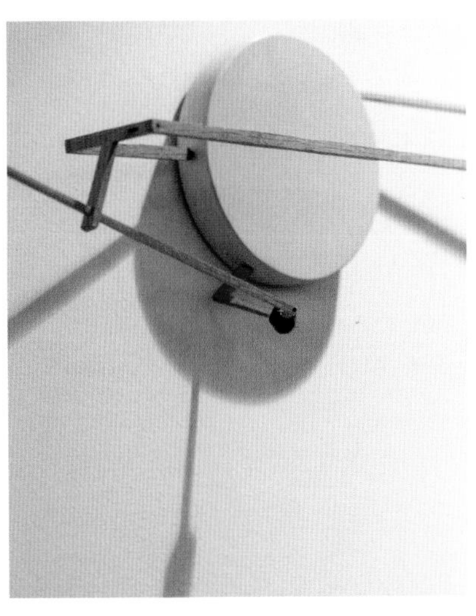

POLLEN STREET SOCIAL

'In 2011, when we launched, we were in the middle of a really bad recession and flexibility was the key idea. In the past, haute cuisine has been all about tasting menus and doing things a certain way, and I felt London was ready for a restaurant where you could still have the standard of cuisine you'd expect in a high-class restaurant but in a setting where you could do what you wanted. So if you wanted to have two starters and a glass of wine you could, or if you wanted three desserts and a pint of beer you could do that. It was always about celebrating British produce, and modern ways of thinking about food, but in a cool, young and happening environment, and not some stuffy old dining room.'

Jason Atherton

PRUFROC
COFFEE
Buono
HARIO
Coffee Syphon
TCA-2
HARIO
Brew Guides —
Woodneck, Syphon
V60 & French Press

PRUFROCK COFFEE

23-25 LEATHER LANE

CAMDEN – LONDON, EC1N 7TE

PRUFROCK COFFEE

Coffee geeks converge at this award-winning coffee bar on Clerkenwell's oh-so-hip Leather Lane for much more than a frothy cappuccino. One of the founders of a new wave of coffee houses with an emphasis on the science behind the perfect cup, the company's manifesto is to 'approach your coffee like a cook'. Highly trained baristas weigh out ingredients, regulate temperatures and use all the latest coffee kit, like Chemex, AeroPresses and syphons, alongside ground-breaking brew methods to create some of London's most delicious coffee. Prufrock also runs a coffee school, which trains professional baristas and enthusiasts in everything from making the perfect espresso to latte art.

BRITISH TERROIR 401

PRUFROCK COFFEE

23-25 LEATHER LANE

CAMDEN – LONDON, EC1N 7TE

ADT
The Quality Chop House
The
94
Dining and Tea
94
92
SNACKS
CLASS CATERER
Q
DINING ROOM

92-94 FARRINGDON ROAD

CAMDEN – LONDON, EC1R 3EA

QUALITY CHOP HOUSE

THE
QUALITY
CHOP
HOUSE
DINING ROOM
WINE BAR & SHOP

Thornback Ray
brown butter, capers,
sea purslane
£16
Longhorn Beef
potato, watercress,
walnuts
Rump 270g £22.50
Rump 480g £42
Sirloin 590g £65
on the bone
Rib 2kg £128
on the bone

In memory of
DAVID HENRY EYRE
26.3.1924 - 13.1.1991

92-94 FARRINGDON ROAD
CAMDEN – LONDON, EC1R 3EA

QUALITY CHOP HOUSE

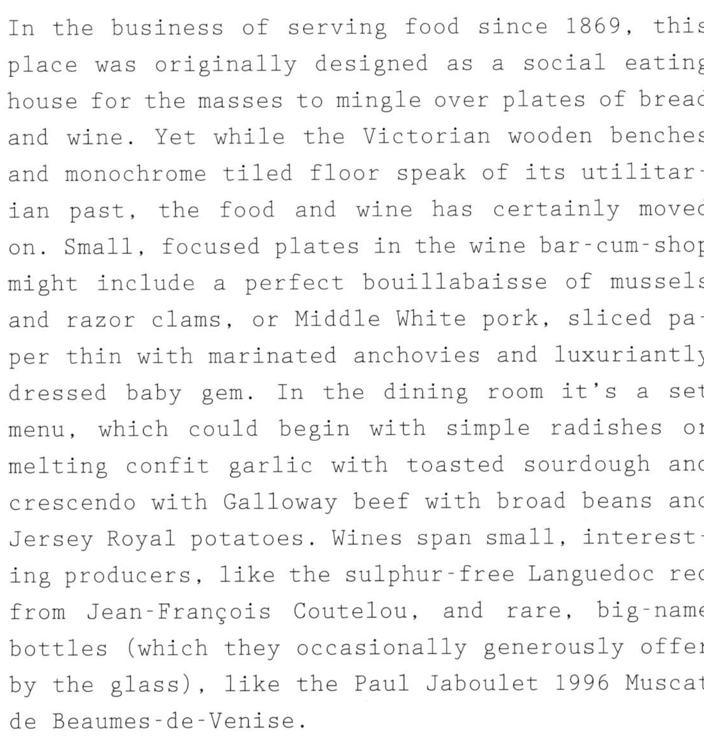

In the business of serving food since 1869, this place was originally designed as a social eating house for the masses to mingle over plates of bread and wine. Yet while the Victorian wooden benches and monochrome tiled floor speak of its utilitarian past, the food and wine has certainly moved on. Small, focused plates in the wine bar-cum-shop might include a perfect bouillabaisse of mussels and razor clams, or Middle White pork, sliced paper thin with marinated anchovies and luxuriantly dressed baby gem. In the dining room it's a set menu, which could begin with simple radishes or melting confit garlic with toasted sourdough and crescendo with Galloway beef with broad beans and Jersey Royal potatoes. Wines span small, interesting producers, like the sulphur-free Languedoc red from Jean-François Coutelou, and rare, big-name bottles (which they occasionally generously offer by the glass), like the Paul Jaboulet 1996 Muscat de Beaumes-de-Venise.

The Rock &
Rock & Sole Plaice
Fish & Chips
Unsuitable for HGVs
47
47
2011
100 YEARS

47 ENDELL STREET

COVENT GARDEN – LONDON, WC2H 9AJ

ROCK & SOLE PLAICE

ROCK & SOLE PLAICE

The great British tradition of fish and chips is thriving in Covent Garden, and it has been since 1871, when a chip shop was first established on this site. The current owners took over in the 1980s and were taught the original frying methods by two old ladies – former employees who'd had the shop in their family for three generations and were keen to preserve its good reputation. And their legacy lives on: queues for takeaway form on a daily basis, but eat in the restaurant you get the benefit of warm service and cosy, casual decor. Choose between rock, sole, halibut, haddock, skate, cod and plaice, slather on the complimentary ketchup and tartar sauce and prepare for the simplest of pleasures: crunching through the light, crispy batter to the moist, flaking fish beneath.

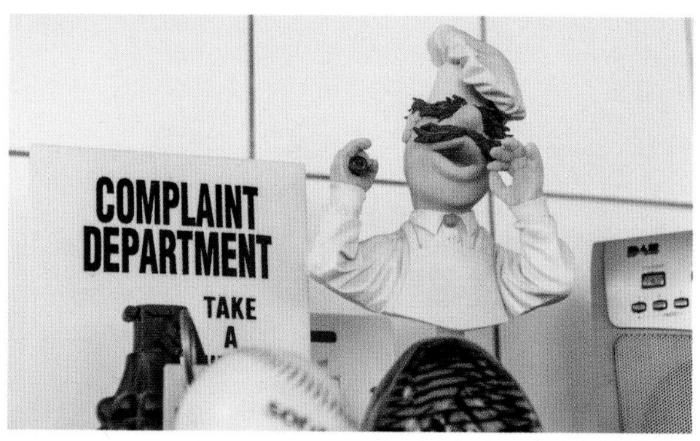

ROCK & SOLE PLAICE

47 ENDELL STREET

COVENT GARDEN – LONDON, WC2H 9AJ

RULES

35 MAIDEN LANE

COVENT GARDEN – LONDON, WC2E 7LB

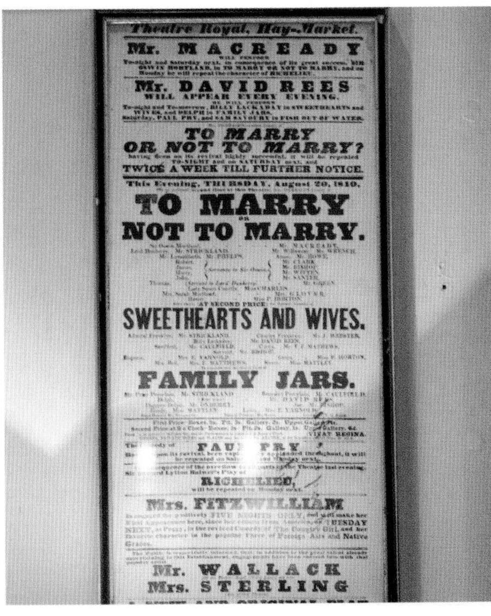

RULES

In the heart of a thriving theatreland, London's oldest restaurant is still going strong. Owned by just three families throughout its 200-year history, Rules is about heritage and tradition taken with a generous helping of fun. A collision of antlers, fixed to the entrance as you walk in, tells of the restaurant's love affair with game, which it sources from its very own estate in the High Pennines. The walls hang with artwork indicative of its cultural significance – having long been a culinary 'green room' for literary, theatre and film figures – and the menus sing with traditional British dishes like steak and kidney suet pudding (with optional oysters). Make sure you make time for a pre- or post-prandial gimlet in its bar upstairs, where there's a silver tray complete with whole Stilton, should you feel the need for cheese at any given moment...

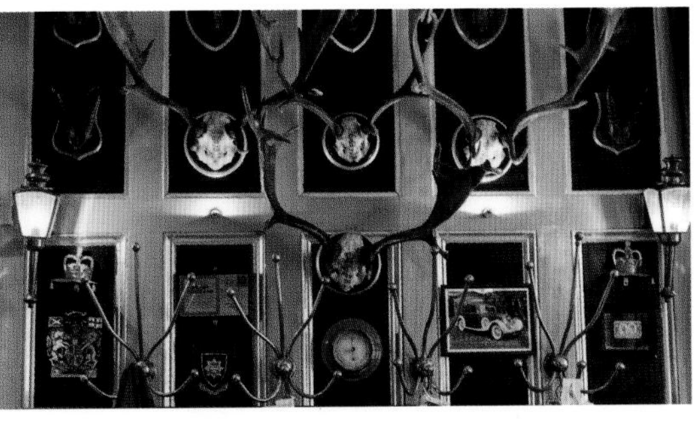

SHED (THE)

122 PALACE GARDENS TERRACE

NOTTING HILL – LONDON, W8 4RT

BRITISH 415 TERROIR

COLMAN'S MU

122 PALACE GARDENS TERRACE

NOTTING HILL – LONDON, W8 4RT

THE SHED

As food-scene buzzwords go, it doesn't get much more 'family-run' or 'farm-to-plate' than this little restaurant in Notting Hill. But far from courting cliché, this place provides a raucous romp into country-style hospitality. Owner brothers the Gladwins have multiple talents they lend to this operation: Richard provides his restaurant management, Oliver, his modern British cooking, and Greg, his farming, which he does from Nutbourne, in the family home of West Sussex, while the other two are based on-site in London. Inside, a pastoral-dining mash-up – including a tractor-bonnet bar, wagon wheels and reclaimed-barrel tables – lend a merry, welcoming setting, while Richard's menus sing like a dawn chorus with British terroir flavours and ingredients. This could mean crab and samphire fritters with chive mayonnaise, followed by fennel-cured pollack with pickled cucumber, radish and lemon, or deep-fried slow-cooked lamb 'chips' with parsley, lemon and harissa. Wines are well selected and interesting, and even include the family's own Sussex Reserve, which is made on the banks of the river Arun.

15-16 BRADBURY STREET

DALSTON – LONDON, N16 8JN

WHITE RABBIT

WHITE RABBIT

Dalston's food scene is still in its embryonic stages, but leading the way is this sceneish side-street eatery, where young maverick chef Danny Rogers is tantalising taste buds from his tumbledown kitchen, complete with makeshift wood oven and indoor barbecue. On reclaimed crates flung with faux-fur throws, as tea lights twinkle and a modish playlist hums, stylish young things sip cocktails from jam jars and fawn over small plates of Rogers' flavour-packed, internationally-inflected food. This could mean an explosively creamy burrata flecked with fennel pollen and lemon rind and slooshed with grassy extra-virgin olive oil, or soft charred aubergine with jewels of pomegranate, ash and thick, sour yoghurt. Unusual cuts are a penchant of the chef, who keeps the menu affordable to his young, local crowd with dishes like lamb belly with miso baba ganoush, spring onion and radish, or pork neck with pickled peach, chicory and almonds. The drinks list is short, accessible and relevant, and features a very slurpable Picpoul de Pinet.

WHITE RABBIT

15-16 BRADBURY STREET

DALSTON – LONDON, N16 8JN

WRIGHT BROTHERS
SOHO OYSTER HOUSE

13 KINGLY STREET

SOHO – LONDON, W1B 5PW

WRIGHT BROTHERS

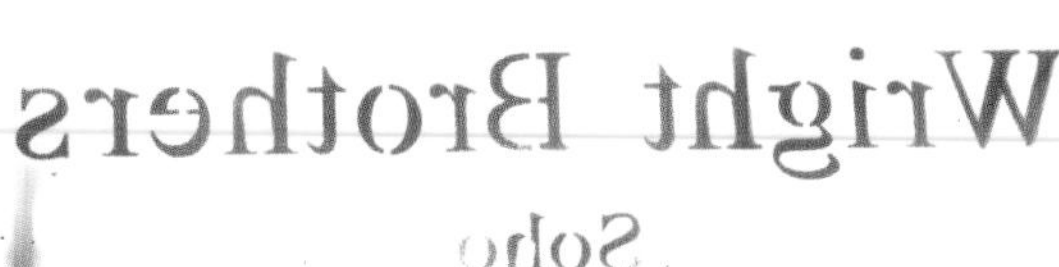
Wright Brothers
Soho

RAW BAR
SPECIALE DE CLAIRE

WRIGHT BROTHERS

When it launched back in 2002 in Borough Market, this oyster wholesaler and now-restaurant group was supplying some of London's top restaurants with French oysters. Over the years though, it's become synonymous with championing and popularising home-grown British oysters from both its own farm on the Helford River in Cornwall and all over the UK, shifting 4 tonnes of the sought-after molluscs a week. A visit to its stylish Soho site reveals a spectacular journey into British tidal terroir, with, depending on the season, a selection of Cornish natives, Dorset rocks, Northumberland Lindisfarne oysters and fresh day-boat fish and shellfish from sustainable stocks.

13 KINGLY STREET

SOHO – LONDON, WIB 5PW

TIME TO
DRINK
CHAMPAGNE
AND DANCE
ON THE
TABLE

THE BODY SHOP
Poundland
£1
COSTA
LS56 XHE

UNDERGROUND
Brixton
Oxford Circus
159
Streatham
DW 59
AT CINEMAS
JUNE 7
ARRIVA
VDL BUS
ARRIVA
LJ04 LFE
Iceland
STARBUCK
great
value
everyday!

CHARING CROSS SW1
WHITEHALL SW1
PRET A MANGER
Freshly prepared • good • natural food
hours a day
SALE 50%

TRAFALGAR STUDIOS
24
MANGO
phs Greenleaf
079 2080 9090

INDEX BY ESTABLISHMENT TYPE

Caffé Concerto
Concerto
Caffé Concerto
Caffé Concerto
Caffé

ACKNOWLEDGEMENTS

J'aime London.
This city welcomed me six years ago, and since then I have never stopped discovering it and admiring its unending creative passion for gastronomy. I am fascinated by the breadth of the city's different cuisines and scenes, which make it such a cosmopolitan and unique place.

Thank you to everybody who has shared their work and their passion with us, whether restaurateurs, chefs, producers, or artisans. They have warmly welcomed me and shared with me their land, products, cuisine and passion.

I would like to thank Rosie Birkett, whose writing talent was of great assistance, and Cécile Rebbot, who helped me to make a difficult selection from all the different places.

Thank you to the designers and editors who took part in this adventure:

- Pierre Monetta, photographer, who understood the city and was able to capture its places and people vividly and up close.
- Pierre Tachon, art director, who once again has turned my intentions for this book into reality.
- Astrid Broders, who masterfully coordinated the making of this book.
- Emmanuel Jirou-Najou, publishing director.
- Alice Gouget, editor-in-chief and head of the publishing team.

I hope you enjoy browsing through this book as much as I enjoyed making it, and that you will feel the urge to discover my London, truly a city for gourmets.

Alain Ducasse